This book is dedicated to my Sue who puts up with me and my crazy car restorations. Of course, I do have to put up with her craziness so I think we are even.

Bob Herzog
5/24/12

To see all my Lotus restoration pictures visit Lotuscorps.org

Europa Euphoria by Bob Herzog Part 1 of?

I wrote a series of articles for our local Lotus Corps newsletter from 1990-1997 when I took two very tired Lotus Ford Cortina junkyard dogs and made one pretty nice car out of them. That car is gone, sold to a collector in Greece. I self published a book out of the collection of articles in case you are interested in reading about it, I still have a couple copies for sale. Since then I finished up a Series 3 Elan restoration that was started by the late Al Kupferschmidt – one of the founding fathers of Lotus Corps. Sold that Elan to a young lady in Chicago who is an Avengers/Emma Peel fan. Emma Peel used to dress in leather and was quite tantalizing to us when we were kids. (She still looks great!) I also fixed up and sold a right hand drive S3 Elan that I was the high ebay bidder (literally) one night after having a few too many beers at a Lotus Corps meeting. I sold that car to a Japanese fellow in Detroit who is eventually going to take the car back home with him to Japan. I also rebuilt a Lotus Seven America from a pile of shrapnel brought up from the Florida Keys. Made a new chassis from scratch myself! I sold that Seven year restoration of a Seven to a buyer in Hong Kong. I finished up a nice Series 2 Elan up at our lake house in my spare time. That one went to a nice guy in Utah. Throughout all those projects since the Cortina, I did not spend any time at the keyboard keeping track of the fun and frivolity that takes place behind the scenes of a restoration. I decided to try this writing thing again and I hope you like the semi humorous toilet humor I try to inject into these semi-technical articles as you sit in your "library" reading.

I was standing at the cross roads in my garage. The Seven was done. The project Elan was up North at the lake house, so I had no real project car to work on in my Des Plaines garage. Every car I owned had 2 coats of wax on them. The lawn looked pretty good and my wife Sue was getting tired of me walking into the house and bugging her. "You need another project" she yelped at me as she slapped my groping hands away from her as she folded the laundry one day. Well you don't have to tell me twice! Not that I'm going to give up perfecting sexual harassment in the home, but I will take her up on the advice to get another project car. I had been keeping an eye on ebay and had scrounged around all the usual web sites looking for another Elan project or maybe old Elite. I wasn't coming up with anything reasonable. There was a wrecked Elan in

Milwaukee and a toasted one in Pennsylvania, but they wanted way too much money for those. Paul Quiniff was willing to sell me the S2 Europa I had sold to him many years ago, but that was way too modified for what I like to do – restore them to stock or better than stock condition. Europa projects are very easy to find, but only the late model Twin Cam Specials are worth anything, even fully restored.

One of Rich Cwik's famous claims is that over the years he has owned 2% of the total Europa production (Perhaps a bit boastful?). That's a lot of fiberglass even if the 10 year production numbers are less than what GM puts out in a week. Rich's current Europa stock included a pure racecar (with one of the best Greg Wisniewski paint jobs you ever saw – inspired by just the right mix of Olympia beer and shots of Southern Comfort); an S2 Renault powered car and a very late model Twin Cam Special with the 5-speed. I was familiar with all three. The Twin Cam was the only one of his collection to move under its own power in the last 20 years. This particular Twin Cam car Rich bought in 1996 and had a horrid florescent green paint job put on it. The green was kind of like a British Racing Green, but it had this additive put in the paint so that it actually glowed in the dark. Rich hauled it out to the Lotus Owners Gathering (LOG) in Ohio and had won the dubious award of the "Europa most needing a new dashboard". As a prize, Rich was handed a brand new wood dashboard only hours after he had purchased a new one at the LOG auto-jumble. Since the LOG, Rich had neglected the car and it was in storage, literally up on a shelf in Jack Buchinger's garage/house (more on that later).

So Rich and I agreed on a price and one Friday afternoon I picked him up in Sue's Audi with my trusty rusty trailer bouncing along, and we headed out to Jack's in Princeton Illinois where the car was stored. When Jack had retired from Illinois Bell/ Ameritech/ SBC/ AT&T, he decided to move out to the boonies, so it took us several hours to get to Jack's place. Rich brought along his cute little pug dog Winston. Winston spent the first hour on Rich's lap snorting up boogars and slobbering all over the passenger window. He finally settled down and went to sleep at Rich's feet. When the car door opened upon arrival at Jack's place, Winston took off running. His sniffer was going crazy taking in all the smells of the farmland. He followed his nose down the road for a few minutes visiting every tree he spotted (or is that spotting every tree he visited?). He then noticed he was waaaaay far away from us, got scared and came scampering back.

Now Jack's house is basically a BIG pole barn. He always wanted a garage that was actually TOO big, if that's possible. So when he started building his dream house in the country, he started out by making his dream garage. The barn appears to be about 120' X 40'. Jack sectioned off about 40' X 40" and made that part into his house. It has a big living room, kitchen, bedrooms and bath. It's an extreme garage with an attached house. As you come in the main door, off to the left is a reproduction model of Rich's old restoration shop. It comes complete with back to back shelving units filled up to the 18' ceiling with tons of "Stuff". Not to be confused of course with what most wives would call junk. As Rich defines it, "Stuff is the Junk that you need and Junk is the Stuff you need to get rid of – or something like that. So when Rich had to close down his shop a few years ago, Jack had this big empty garage that Rich just kept bringing truckload after trailer load after van load of "Stuff" until it was packed quite full. Packed just like Rich's old shop. The middle part of Jack's building is Jack's actual garage where he has essentials such as the hydraulic lift and a huge electric forklift. He also has a wall-o-cars. Actually, they are mostly Rich's cars. Jack has his new Nissan 350-Z on the lift and his old Nissan tube-frame road racer on the lower shelf and then there's Rich's 3 Europas. Soon to be only 2 at least here. Rich has other storage that no one else alive has ever seen. There is supposed to be a couple more cars there including an old Lotus Super Seven.

After a quick tour of the shop, we spent about 45 minutes moving Jack's stuff (not junk, see definition above) around so we could maneuver the forklift over to the shelf to bring down the Europa. We managed to get it down without dropping it on Winston and we rolled it out onto my waiting trailer. Pretty dirty but apparently complete. Rich tossed in a couple new items like a dashboard, stainless steel door hinges, a header, a different intake manifold and a New Old Stock carpet set. Our stomachs were growling (yes it was a very loud chorus) so we headed into town for a Friday Night Fish Fry. The buzzing metropolis of downtown Princeton was just down the road a piece. Actually, it's a fairly big town now because they recently got their own McDonalds AND a Wal-Mart! Winston stayed in the Audi as we parked next door to the restaurant at the Tractor and Trailer store. I had to leave the doors unlocked as Winston was setting off the inside motion detector alarm on the Audi. Jack said not to worry, there was no crime in Princeton and nobody was going to steal Winston. The Friday Fish Fry crowd was a gathering of all the farmers and workers throughout the area. Jack talked to some folks he knew as the farmers flirted with the waitresses. Pretty good fish fry at a real cheap price.

   The ride home was a bit challenging as it was raining pretty good and there was a good wind going. At least some of the dirt got rinsed off the Europa. I made it home by midnight and just backed the whole car/trailer/Europa thing into the yard to be unloaded the next day.

Europa Euphoria by Bob Herzog Part 2 of?

4/4/2005, disassembly time! Lot's of people ask me how many hours I put into a restoration. It seems like thousands, but I never really kept track on the other projects I've done so this time I've got a little clip board and I'll see how long it takes for each phase of the operation.

This Europa was assembled at the factory in June of 1973; therefore it is the Newest Lotus I have ever worked on. That being said, it is still 32 years old and I'm sure I will find mostly very crusty and rusty parts in this phase of restoration. The engine/trunk cover (in the back) was the first part to come off and get shoved up into the garage attic. I put all the little nuts and bolts for the cover in a little butter dish. I use separate butter dishes marked with component names on masking tape for each major chunk of the car. That way when I go to re-assemble the car many moons later, I can narrow down what goes where. Since this is the first butter dish, I also dated it. It's kind of interesting when I get to the point of putting those first nuts and bolts back on the car, I find out how many years and months it took to get back to these first parts. My 1965 Elan project car took me 2 ½ years to get back to the drivers door butter dish. I usually clean up and re-use most of the bolts and install all new washers and locknuts. The Lotus Seven that I did was so bad that I didn't use butter dishes. Almost everything was junk so I threw out almost all the bolts as well as the nuts.

I took off the Stromberg carbs and manifold and a few other items in the engine bay without any problem. The fiberglass body is held onto the chassis with about a dozen bolts 2X2X2X2X2X2 from front to rear. The first two I looked at in the engine bay sit in a little lip that conveniently holds all the water and muck that happens to get in the engine bay. The bolt heads are also only half-height so when I attempted to unbolt those first two body bolts, it became quickly apparent that this would be the first of many jobs for the sawz-all/ air grinder/air cut-off tools. Sparks were a flying!

The front trunk came off with ease as did all the little paraphernalia and wiring in the front trunk compartment. The radiator is located up front and that gave me a bit of trouble. 32 years of weathering had caused the nuts to be rusted on stronger than the tensile strength of the old brazing that held the bolts onto the radiator housing. Snap-snap-snap. 3 broke off. Only 1 out of 4 actually unscrewed. The part of the radiator housing that held the water was fine but there is a heavy mesh screen that goes over the part of the radiator that is exposed to the wheel well. That heavy mesh was now more like a heavy Mush. This will be a real challenge for my favorite radiator shop, later in the project.

    The driver's door had a new stainless steel hinge assembly so it was not rusted to death. It was a bit stubborn however. I was just able to reach inside the door twist the rod back and forth and back and forth. After about a half hour of that my hands were really red and sore. After looking at the new hinge kits sitting on my workbench, I then realized that the bottom of the hinge had a threaded hole. I drilled out the rivets holding the aluminum sill cover and exposed the hole in the body where the hinge shaft comes out. I jacked up the car and threaded in a bolt to use with a vice-grip and a hammer. Ideally it would have been nice to put the car on a lift and use a slide hammer, but you have to get by with the tools you have. I was able to hammer the shaft out. After unhooking the power window wires, I was able to get the drivers door off and set it on the workbench. The passenger side was a bit easier because I had the routine now. Only this time I wasn't paying full attention as I pulled and tapped out the hinge shaft. I was sweating pretty good and as the shaft was just about to pop out, the whole door popped out and fell on my head. Luckily Europa doors don't have steel I-beams for occupant protection. Luckily I've got a pretty hard head. It still smarted pretty good. How come when you drop something on your head it smarts? Shouldn't it stupid instead of smart?

    That was enough for one night so I closed up and headed into the house. Only then did I realize how sore my hands really were from twisting that shaft inside the door. My fingers were now swollen like little sausages and after I washed my dirty hands they looked like they had been stuck in scalding hot water. I got out a couple ice cubes to soak them and a couple cold beers to rinse things out internally as I sat down and chilled out in front of the TV.

Europa Euphoria by Bob Herzog Part 3 of?

Time to Get Gooey. The window frame is held onto the door with two small self-tapping screws and lots of really gooey black tar type adhesive. Of course I didn't really know this at first so I didn't put on any rubber gloves. I took out my utility knife and started cutting away at the goop. Then I started scraping it with a screwdriver. Finally I got out the big putty knife and scraped out enough so I could pry out the window frame. Even though the glue was 32 years old, it was still a gooey mess. I scraped off the excess and then used some paint thinner and rags to clean up what was left.

Since my hands were pretty goopy, I decided to attack the windshield, which was also held in with the same goopy glue. They used so much goop on the windshield that I could scrape up a big wad of it at a time and fling it into the garbage can. Only it was so goopy that it didn't want to come off my hand. I'd take it off one hand with the other and then it would get stuck to that hand. It was like one of those old Three Stooges routines (no Curley references please!). I had to reach into the garbage can and find some old paper to grab the goop to get it off my hand. Yuck! Couple this with the fact that it was 85 degrees in the garage and I was sweating pretty profusely. It's a challenge to wipe the sweat off your forehead (or in my case, a fivehead) with the only part of you that is not covered with sticky goo; which are your elbows. It took about 45 minutes of scraping and working on the windshield to get it out. After that it took another half hour of cleaning to get the windshield clean enough to grab and put up in the garage attic. My hands looked like I had just sealed an asphalt driveway with my bare hands. Even after soaking and wiping them down with lacquer thinner, they were still a mess. Oh, and that automotive lacquer thinner lets you know if you have any cuts or open sores!

Next trip to the garage was spent cleaning the goop off the area on the body that the windshield had set in. The rubber strip that held the inside interior in place had so much black goop in it that it hung down like it was held by black spider webs. The rubber door seals also had the goop all over them. This goop was so sticky that you couldn't really scrape it off. The scraper would just smear it and get stuck on the scrapper. Lot's of lacquer thinner with paper towels and old rags were used here. You know the routine. For the first swipes you reach into the garbage can and grab some already pretty dirty rags or paper towels or used Kleenex, soak them in lacquer thinner and use them first to knock down the big chunks. Then you use the "not as dirty" paper towels or rags soaked in lacquer thinner. There are different stages of dirt and grease depending on the job at hand. Just like clothes. You have your regular good clothes. When you wear those you should not even walk towards the workbench or project car. Dirt just jumps off the workbench onto your belly. Your wife will say, "What's that?" and you'll say what's what?" because you can't see it around the bend of your belly. That's also a part of what's known as Over the Hill! Next level down from your clean clothes is the first level of grubbies. First level is what you wear when you wash the car, mow the lawn and do light garage and project car restoration work. You can wear them to go to the hardware store, but not really to any other public places. The next level down is your super grubbies that you use when you are going to de-grease an engine, do a brake job, re-pack wheel bearings or greet your mother-in-law. The problem with any of the grubbies is that your significant other always seems to want to throw them out rather than wash them. So you are left standing in front of your dresser in your undies, wondering what clothes need to graduate to the next level of dirt. This is just an evil plot by the significant other to get you to go out and buy new clothes. Being a male, you'd much rather spend your hard earned cash on some new (or used) Lotus parts or at least a case of beer. You only go get new clothes when you run out of old clothes to wear because the significant other has tossed them out and you have unwittingly put them out on the curb with the trash. If you've been married a while, the wife even learns that she has to hide the old clothes at the bottom of the garbage can. If she puts them near the top, the male will sniff them out and take them back in the house, immediately put them on and exclaim, "How could you throw out my favorite sweatshirt?"

  So anyway, I got all the black goop cleaned up and after scrubbing my hands with lacquer thinner and orange goop hand cleaner I had most of the big chunks cleaned off. It just looked like I had black eyeliner on my fingernails for the next week. That and the skin on my hands were white from the lacquer thinner drying them out.

  Next up or off so to speak were the seats. On an Elan, you simply unbolt the two front bolts that hold the hinges in place. The big meaty bolts are screwed into bobbins that are glassed into the floor.

Look underneath an Elan and you can see the bobbins. You can also tilt the Elan seat forward. Europas however are different. There are two sliding seat rails screwed into the seat and the mating part of the seat rails are screwed into hidden bobbins in the floor. The bottom of a Europa is smooth with no screws or bobbin heads sticking out. The problem here is that you cannot really get at the screws with the seat in its normal position. There are two bolts in the front and two in the rear. The theory here is that you release the slider latch and slide the seat all the way forward and when the top of the seat just about reaches the windshield area, the whole seat lifts out. This is fine on a car that has been used regularly. The problem arises when the seat gets rusted in place, as was the case here. Rusted real bad. Couldn't move them. Couldn't get at the screws. What to do? I opened up a "thinking" beer and spent some time poking, prying, banging and thumping, but to no avail. I had a big crowbar, a small crowbar, a regular hammer, a small sledgehammer, a slide hammer, screw drivers – nothing was budging the seat. During the course of all this as I was sweating profusely all over the place. I had the trouble light on the interior floor with the top of my head squished down on the floor and my sweaty forehead smashed against the seat cushion to get a close up look at the rust to see if I could see what to do. I then realized that a lot of stinky sweaty butts and crotches had sat on that old rotten seat over the last 32 years. I placed an old t-shirt/rag on the seat to keep those old stinky butt cooties off of me.

   I managed to get one of the front bolts unscrewed by jamming a screwdriver in the seat rail against the bolt head and unscrewing the nut. The other side wouldn't budge but the rusty seat rail began to split so I just ripped that corner off. The two back bolts were inaccessible but now the seat wiggled at least a little bit on one side. I took the 4-foot handle from my floor jack and pried on the seat back and got a little more wiggle. After about 30 minutes more of wiggling, twisting, thumping and sweating, the seat finally slid forward and I pulled it out. Tucked in the back of the rotted carpet I found the remains of a mouse nest and some chewed up acorns. At least there was no evidence of the deceased resident rodents. That seat was on the Passenger side, which was easier than the one I just pulled out.

   The driver's side rails were really stuffed full of rotted carpet mung. I had a hard time even jamming a screwdriver into the rails.

I ended up just ripping both front bolts out. It split the rails. I'll either have to find new ones or do some welding work here. The seat still would not budge. No amount of prying, twisting or banging would give me the slightest sign of a wiggle. I ended up pulling off the vinyl and pulling apart the seat to get access at the two remaining nuts which are welded to the seat rails. Now I couldn't get even a finger underneath to the bolt head, but now I could at least get at the corresponding nut. I decided to try and tighten instead of loosen to see if I could break the bolts rather than unscrew them. They were fine thread and pretty good grade, so the air gun wouldn't break them. I put a long pipe on my breaker bar and after a turn and a half of really tough pushing, one snapped off. Surprisingly, I did not mash my knuckles on anything! The other nut/bolt wouldn't succumb to the tightening strategy, it just spun. So I managed to fit the air cut off tool in there and cut the bolt into pieces until it all came off. I had to keep the sparks under control as the old seat and carpet was as close to spontaneous combustion kindling as you can get. Finally, after about 4 hours of beating, banging, prying, twisting, cutting, tearing, swearing, sweating and bleeding, both seats were sitting on to the floor of my garage, their rusty undersides and rotting foam exposed for the first time in 32 years. I went in the house and cleaned up in the slop sink (excuse me, my significant other prefers that I call that the laundry tub) before I got into the bathtub. As I was striping down for the tub, my wife came in and remarked – what happened? She pointed to my knees, which were beet red from my kneeling on the throw rug in the garage (my garage rug is also known as the Polish creeper). I guess red knees are just a normal by-product of all the kneeling and praying that takes place when working on an old British car.

Europa Euphoria by Bob Herzog Part 4 of?

I've worked for the phone company for over 36 years and we have acronyms for everything. I had a real rough day in the garage the other day and I decided to put some acronyms together to try and classify what kind of day I had. Most people know what RPM and MPG stand for. Here are some new ones.

You know it's going to be a bad day if your F-COD is < 10:00 AM. You feel like you have really cut a path through the jungle if your CPD is > 5. At the time it's awful, but you usually look back, point and laugh for every STFOOMF you get. A BMFNB is worse than scraping fingernails on a chalkboard. But really the worst is if you get a major PDM.

F-COD stands for First Cut Of the Day. It's a Saturday. You get your chores done early; wash the car, go to the bank, go to the Post Office, service the wife and mow the lawn. Not necessarily it that order of course. So you are done with the chores and now you have time to work on your favorite project in the garage. I had a bad Saturday the other day when after finishing my chores I went for some aspirin in the medicine cabinet only to notice that a good bit of blood was drooling down the back of my hand. So instead of just getting aspirin for my sore back, I had to clean up my hand in the slop sink enough so the band-aid would stick. Now here is another thing I want to point out. Why do they make and why do women buy those teeny, tiny little band-aids? You know the ones. They're so small you have a hard time opening them because your fingers are so much bigger than they are. These things would be fine for a cut on a mouse or maybe an ant, but not for any kind of cut that a real man would bother to try and stop the bleeding with. If I have a cut that small, I don't even bother with it, unless it's real small in diameter but maybe 2 inches deep. You know, like an ice pick wound, or maybe something from a stray nail gun shot. Maybe then I would use those fairy band-aids. What we real men need are Man-Daids, something a couple inches in diameter with enough gauze padding to do some real soaking up. But at least I make the effort to find proper, clean stuff to tend to my wounds. I've seen some of my old-timer neighbors with their entire finger wrapped up with black electrical tape. I ask if the tape was just to stop the bleeding or if it was holding the chopped off piece of appendage in place. They usually don't want to answer.

So I sorted through all the fairy band-aids and put a Man-Daid on my F-COD and headed back out to the garage and start on the real work. Today's project is to take out the dash in the Europa. Real easy on an Elan, Royal pain in the butt on a Europa. After finding hidden rivets and nuts on the console, I managed to pull the console out without tearing the 32-year-old ABS plastic. The dash itself had all sorts of extra supports. The Elan is a real flexi flyer. When you go through a turn in an Elan, the wood dash flexes and creaks with the turn. On a Europa there are all sorts of extra braces to tie everything to the body. Almost like they thought the wood dash would add stiffness to the body. So I continue to unbolt and unscrew and drill out bits and pieces that hold the dash in place. On this day I had to stop several times during the project to swear at inanimate objects and stick the bleeding part of me in my mouth and go find additional Man-Daids. At least the cuts weren't real bad and the parts were relatively clean.

This particular Europa dash removal job was especially nasty. I had started out with my F-COD at about 10:30, by the end of the day my CPD (Cuts Per Day) was at 5 and to top it off, whilst releasing the grip of my vice grips I got a real good PDM (Pinched Da Meat). It was a tough day. Could be worse. Sometimes as I'm talking to my buddy Paul Quiniff I will notice evidence of a real good Smashed the **** Out Of My Finger (STFOOMF). Sometimes he laughs, sometimes not, depending on how many pain killing Old Styles he has had since the incident. Another thing to watch out for, but luckily I haven't had in a long time is a BMFNB. I keep my fingernails cut pretty short because a broken fingernail is WAY better than a "Bent My Finger Nail Back". O-o-o-o, that gives me the willies just thinking about it.

Only once in my life did I have to go to the emergency room because of a cut. On that occasion I was working with my brother-in-law Gregski on some stubborn Elan rear shock inserts that did not want to come out. Greg was pushing and I was holding or the other way around, I don't remember. All I know was that the palm of my left hand was the recipient of the sharp end of the big screwdriver. It went in pretty deep and was bleeding pretty good. I stuck the bleeding part in my mouth and knew I had a problem when I had to go - gulp! But I digress....

Europa Euphoria by Bob Herzog Part 5 of?

Once in a while in the disassembly stage you have to do a bit of clean up. Since I had just ripped (literally) the seats out, it was time to take the shop vac out to get rid of all the rotted carpets and mouse mung. However, before I did that, I wanted to take advantage of one of the few times you get some of your investment back in a project car. Although this is a very, very small portion back – every little bit helps. So I took a screwdriver and rooted around in the carpet fragments and found 96 cents in old crusty coins. Hey, enough to cover a toll in Illinois! As I started cleaning further and taking out more bits in the interior, I found more and more coins. Some tucked under the seat rails, some stuck in the console, and some slid behind the carpet in the back. All in all, I think I got about $3.00 in grubby coins. I used to save all my pennies just so I could use them in the tollbooths to make things more difficult for the toll-way system. Nothing against toll-way people personally. I just think the concept of having everyone stop every couple miles to throw in coins is ridiculous! It wastes gas, time and pollutes to boot. Since they started letting you get through with the I-pass, it's not so bad. I still wonder how much is spent just to support itself. Oh well – our government in in-action. Now I'll have to take the coins to the bank with the rest of the change I put in an old road racing trophy/mug/jar every night. Funny how certain trophies bring back memories. I got this particular 2nd place trophy from a Midwest council road race back in 1980. I used to race a 1970 Cortina GT. My recollection of the race was that I didn't stick around for the trophies so our club president accepted it and handed it to me next spring at our annual medical examination. Midwest Council racing requires all drivers go through a medical check up annually and since they actually had a few doctors in the club, they arranged to have a February meeting where the Doctors would do the physical check up for free. Everyone would show up at the Pres's house with a case of beer. We'd take numbers; sit down to watch either porn or videos of car crashes while we waited our turn to see one of the Docs. The Docs would always complain that everyone's blood pressure was high! So anyway, I'm paying my dues and signing up for the medical examination and the Pres hands me my trophy mug, a nice ceramic

17

mug with a drawing of Blackhawk Farms raceway on the side. A nice mug and I really liked it. The part that I didn't like was that it was full of his and everyone else's cigarette butts – Yuck. Nice trophy presentation. So the mug is clean now of course, I just flashback to that moment in time when I see it. But I digress...

As you disassemble a project car, you take a mental inventory of what parts are good (if any), what parts need to be rebuilt (most everything) and which ones are completely trash or missing. Some are major, some very small. Sometimes the small ones are the details that make a restoration special. With my Lotus Seven project, one of the highlights was finding a very nice pair of Windgard taillights at a reasonable price. One of the low points of that restoration was when I attached those taillights to the fenders and they both cracked when I tightened the screws because they were so brittle! On this Europa, I could see that the wheels were missing the little plastic center caps. They are only about 2 inches in diameter and not usually noticed by most people but just another detail that I would be looking to take care of. I already found one (need 4 total) on ebay. Cost me $42 for that little bugger. Now I only need 3 more. The good thing about selling junk on ebay and putting the proceeds into a Paypal account is it gives you play money for buying more stuff. Sometimes selling the old junky parts is a way of partially financing the new parts. It's like trading them in on new models. If you sell junk at a good price, it kind of gives you justification in your own mind, to spend too much on other stuff. Notice that you sell junk and buy stuff.

One of the slightly bigger items that I have to deal with is the radiator. The one I have is complete. It's also completely rusty. A radiator shop guy is selling new aluminum Europa radiators for $355 on ebay. They look real slick. I would probably spend at least $150 getting this old one repaired so I think I'll pick up the aluminum one and sell the old one on ebay.

Attaching seatbelts in a fiberglass car is always a challenge. On a Europa, the inside belts are bolted through the inside of the body to the chassis. No problem there, they unbolted fairly easily. The outside belts however just go through the fiberglass to some steel plate that is bolted inside the body. Of course, after 32 years of humidity and water, that steel is just crusty rust. So as I unscrewed the belts, I got a lot of crunch, crunch, crunch noises and the floor became littered with rust dust. I had to take the grinder and grind off all the rusty bolt heads holding the plate in place. I also had to use the saws-all to chop off the seat belt bolt. That seat belt bolt was pretty stubborn too. Once I ground off all the bolts, I could then fish out the remaining fragments of the support plate inside the sill. For the first time I realized that the Europa body is not a one-piece unit. There is a bottom part that is bolted and riveted to the top piece. That's why the rust from the plate was falling on my shoes. It was falling out of the crack where the two body parts are riveted together. When I fished out as much as I could, I shoved the shop vac hose into the sill from the rear wheel well and vacuumed out all the remaining debris. I'll have to fiberglass in some new seat belt supports later. I then used the grinder to take off what was left of interior screws that at one time held in the carpets.

Rich had already replaced the rusty old steel twin gas tanks with new aluminum ones. He said the original left one had a rust hole in the top big enough to put your hand through. And the original right one had a big hole in the bottom. So $680 later, he had a new set of tanks from England. You drill out the fiberboard access panels in the wheel wells and then just unbolt the 4 bolts holding each tank in place. The only issue is the body has to be 4 feet in the air to get the tanks to slide out the bottom. I just left them loose for later when I would pull the body off. Getting close to that milestone.

A final bit of grinding was needed to remove the bolts that held on what I would call some body stiffening rods. These rods connected up to where the top seat belt mounts would go and the other end connected to the rear shocks. Kind of tied the whole car together I guess. Plenty of rust on those babies. Only one unbolted a bit before it snapped off. The others were too rusty to get any grip on them so I had to grind them all off. Now everything is stripped out of the body. Later on during the week I would regret not having worn long sleeves as I did all the grinding. I had worn a dust mask, earplugs and a face shield, but the grinding of rusty metal impregnated little steel trails into my arm and hands. As I scratched those little sores, eventually the metal bits worked their way out but I looked like I had chicken pox for a week.

Europa Euphoria by Bob Herzog Part 6 of?

Well, it was getting about time to pull the body off. Always a momentous occasion, you work real hard to get to that point and when it happens, you reveal if the chassis will require just a little bit of welding or if you have a piece-o-crap on your hands. I had gone over the car several times to make sure all the cables and hoses and bolts and stuff that keep the body in place had been removed. The Europa body is fairly light. Two robust males can usually grunt it up and maneuver it about. I pulled up on the back end and it creaked and moaned a bit but eventually gave up its 32 year old position. I plopped it back down and tried the front. This was a little more stubborn so I employed a hydraulic jack with a big wood plank across the bottom side of the nose. I jacked it up and it made all sorts of creaking noises but finally started to come loose just as the front tires were about to leave the ground. It didn't sound right so I double-checked everywhere to make sure I hadn't left some bolts in place. Everything looked ok so I wedged a two by four between the chassis and the body. I went back to the back and lifted there. It took some balancing finesse to lift the car body, hold it up with a knee whilst I placed a couple two by fours between the chassis and body at the back. I went back to the front and tried to jack up the body some more but it started making some "The fiberglass is tearing somewhere" noises. I found that the steering column was wedged between the rack and the body so I pulled that out. Still the body was protesting. After searching around I found that inside the body behind where the heater core was placed, was a pivot arm for the parking brake. I had unbolted the arm but had neglected to unhook it from the parking brake cable. The pivot arm was still attached and therefore was slicing its way trough the very thin fiberglass that makes up the interior hump. It had wedged itself pretty good so it took a bit of smacking with proper leverage tools (BFH and a BFS) to release the pivot arm and unhook the cable. Once this was done, the front part of the body then moved freely. I started again at the rear to lift and add more two by fours. My intent here was to make sure the body was up high enough and absolutely clear before I got some help with moving the body to a rolling stand. Experience has shown me that if you just get a bunch of guys to help you lift the body and something is still holding the body in place, several things may/will happen. A. Everyone hurts their backs trying to lift the body with the chassis and engine still attached. B. Whatever was still holding the body on will rip, tear or bend. C. Everyone will reach down, count to three and stand up holding bits of fiberglass in their hands that they have ripped off all four corners. D. All of the above. I didn't want that to happen as this Europa body was pretty good, not (yet) needing any fiberglass work. I found that Rich had made up some nice Aeroquip hoses to go to the nice aluminum gas tanks on each side of the body. That hose was keeping the back end from going any further. I placed drain pans under each tank and unbolted the lines from the tanks. Only a little slosh of gas left in each, but it was enough to leave that lovely perfume smell that gasoline has all over my hands and arms. Later that night, even after lots of go-jo hand cleaner and a good shower when I wrapped my loving arms tenderly around my lovely wife in bed she would coo to me in her tender, loving way: "What the Hell is that awful smell on you"?

Everything was clear now. I had wedged in enough two by fours so the body was up about 8 inches off the chassis. My buddy Paul was limping around with a back brace on, the result of a long weekend in the small, back jump seat of a pick-up truck (and yes, alcohol was involved) so I didn't bother him. I rolled out a suitable cart and called my son John and wife Sue to help with the official move. John and I lifted and Sue made sure the cart was in position. A couple of grunts and a bit of re-positioning and it was Miller time!

Paul came by later with some of his back medicine (Old-Styles) and we celebrated the first milestone in this restoration. I got out my clip board where I had been tracking my hours and counted up all the ½ hour, ¾ hour, 2 hr, 2 ½ hr entries over the past 6 months. Because the medicine Paul shared with me was starting to kick in, it took a while to add up the numbers and fractions of numbers. It had been a pretty busy summer so from April 4th when I first got the car through October 10th, I had logged only 55 total hours. This was to completely strip out the interior and exterior of the body and lift it off the chassis. Is this a lot or a little, it doesn't matter since I don't expect to be charging by the hour. But maybe, just maybe if the car turns out really nice I can get 10 cents and hour…

Europa Euphoria by Bob Herzog Part 7 of?

I decided to start stripping the paint off the body and get it in primer before I started on the mechanical bits. This had more to do with the weather than anything else. Fall was upon us and it was getting dark early. Soon it would be cold and I'd be turning on the garage heater. I prefer to do the bodywork outside as it keeps the dust outside. I figured I could work outside only a few more months before snow would get in the way. So one evening after din-din, even though it was dark outside I plopped the hood onto a plastic garbage can in the back yard, donned a suitably old sweatshirt, dust mask and earplugs and started at it with the Dual Action 6" air sander. As I was leaving the house for the garage I told Sue to say goodbye to the sweatshirt. She knew that once I start on the bodywork portion of a project, that sweatshirt will get thinner and holier as the days and nights progressed. Yes, it will be washed periodically, but by the time the project is done, so is the sweatshirt.

The paint came off surprisingly easy and the hood, doors and trunk lid were very straight. Whoever had done the bodywork for Rich had done a real nice job. It was just the final paint that was pretty awful. In two hours I had the paint knocked off of the big flat surfaces of the hood, trunk and doors and began the hand sanding of the corners, edges and crevices. Took about 4 hours total for the parts.

I tackled the main body on a Saturday morning. Just started at one end with the D/A and worked my way around. I would stop every hour to blow my face off with some air, blow my nose, (check the Kleenex to see how much is getting past the mask) go get some fresh air and water. My hands would feel like they were buzzing from the sander vibrations. After about 5 hours I walked on down to Paul's to take a break. We grabbed a cold one and chatted while watching 6 Mexicans across the alley hand-pour a garage foundation. I guess they saved a lot of money by mixing the sand, water and concrete mix by hand rather than just having the concrete truck come in and pour what they needed. Sure looked like back breaking work to us though. They would bring in a pickup truck full of sand, a truck full on concrete mix and between the 6 of them, they had a concrete mixing party. Way too much work for Paul and I, especially with our bad backs. But then again, I have no problem sanding down the Europa boady instead of taking it to a body shop.

After a few "chillin out" beverages with Paul, I went back to the garage, put the mask back on, put in the ear plugs and blew the garage out with the leaf blower. Always makes it look like the garage is on fire with all the dust blowing out the doors.

The next day I finished up the sanding, blew everything out again and then hosed the parts and the body off outside. I hosed out all the undersides of the wheel wells, the front trunk and engine bay to get all the dirt out so that after I paint, I could spray all those hidden areas with black truck bed liner paint later. Total time to get the body ready for touch up Bondo and spot putty was about 16 hours. Not bad at all.

There where a few scratches and dings in the body but not bad at all. Wherever I found a ding, I would dig them out a bit and sand them before applying a bit of Bondo. Some of the edges in the front trunk area had some air bubble pockets. Original from the factory, but I spent a little time grinding them out, applying a bit of Bondo to plug them up and smooth things out. The only fiberglass work I had to do was to plug up the antenna hole that someone had put in the rear quarter. Paul brought home a Fiberglass Field Repair kit from his shop. To plug a hole, you use a grinder with an 80-grit disc to feather the edges on both sides so that the glass tapers down. You cut out new glass to fit the hole and then a bigger one to overlap the hole for each side. Mix up the resin and catalyst; brush on the mixture onto both sides of the hole using a cheap China bristle brush. If you try to use a polyester brush, it dissolves in the resin. Place the fiberglass pieces on a piece of cardboard (a beer can box is perfect). Brush a thick coat of the mixture onto the fiberglass and work it in real good so the glass is saturated. Place the small piece on the hole and the bigger pieces on either side. Coat and soak in more mixture onto the fiberglass. I had to make up a little supporting fixture to keep the glass attached while it cured. A butter dish lid supported by a garden stick worked just fine. The plastic lid pops off easily once everything is dry.

Since the car body was a bit cold, the resin didn't want to kick, so I snuck into the house and borrowed my wife's hairdryer. (Never use one of those on myself.) I hit the hole with a little heat on both sides for about 5 minutes and then let the chemical reaction take over. In an hour it was ready for sanding and a wisp of Bondo. Sue always wonders why her hair dryer smells funny whenever I do fiberglass work.

On a clear Saturday morning I cleaned out the garage and wiped down the body and parts one more time. I had the garage heater cooking so that everything was nice and warm. Paint likes warm. It's allergic to the cold. It breaks out in bubbles and doesn't spray or dry properly. The hood, trunk and doors have to sit on something to be sprayed. For the final paint I hang them from the garage ceiling with bent up coat hangers, but for primer, I just set them on something. I usually go out back and grab a couple of garbage cans to be used as horizontal surfaces. After washing them down, I usually throw a clean old carpet over them just to keep dust from flying up and hitting the painted surface as I spray away. My carpets were pretty dirty. If I use towels, the spray can blow the towel and it may flap against the fresh paint, (learned that the hard way) so I looked at couple of old t-shirts in the rag bin and scratched my head. The next step was rather depressing. I found out that my old t-shirts DO fit over the garbage cans!!! Being barrel chested is OK, being garbage can gutted is not. Well at least I had to stretch them quite a bit to fit over the cans.

So I mixed up some primer, donned my good Darth Vader mask and started to spray. I think I had the pressure a bit high because there was **a lot** of overspray when I was done. I shot one coat on all the edges followed by two full coats on everything. Took about an hour and a half. As I was just finishing up, I could see Paul looking in through the garage window. He told me later that the overspray in the air was so thick he couldn't see me, but he could hear the gun spraying so he knew I was still alive in there. I came out and had a few suds with Paul while waiting for the paint to set. Primer doesn't take long to dry but we needed an excuse to sit and drink. Mind you not much of an excuse is ever needed.

I let everything dry for an hour, opened the door and blew everything out with the leaf blower. As all the dust came flying out the doors it again looked like the garage was on fire. I'm lucky nobody has ever called the fire department on me.

Europa Euphoria by Bob Herzog Part 8 of?

Here's something weird that happened in the garage. I have a built in garage furnace. In the winter, when I'm not around, I keep the garage thermostat set at just above freezing – like 40 degrees. I do this by having a modified thermostat; one that I had taken my Dremel tool to the left side and ground out the plastic stop so I could turn the setting way down. So anyway, I don't let my garage freeze so the cans of paint won't go bad. But when I do go out to the garage and turn up the heat you can hear the cans of paints going "Boink" when they start to warm up. The gasses inside don't like the change in temperature and so they expand and contract. So one evening when I was working in the garage as it was warming up I heard the familiar "Boink" and didn't think anything about it. Later on however I noticed a big puddle of reddish stuff next to the tire of the Elan. I didn't put two and two together right away so I approached the spill and peered down at it. Suddenly I realized what had happened as several drops of red primer dripped onto the back of my neck from the shelf above. A ten year old can of red oxide primer had split a seam and sprung a leak. What a mess spilt paint makes! It's also not easy to get off the back of your neck. I had my son go after the stain on my neck with some lacquer thinner. Yow, that's stronger than aftershave.

Back to work on the Europa, I began to sand down the primer. Now you don't just go around and start willy-nilly sanding. Now's the time to make sure everything is flat and all the little pin holes that show up in primed fiberglass are plugged up. I like to use a paint stick wrapped up in 220 grit paper for this phase. I take "Sticky" and run it across all the flat surfaces in a cross hatch pattern looking for dips and high spots. Use your hand to feel any big valleys or peaks in between sanding. Sticky can also be used for large curves such as the front fenders. For the small tight areas and corners, I use the sanding sponge wrapped in 220 as well. The sponge is purposely made by 3M for sanding. It ensures that overly aggressive sanding fools don't leave finger marks as they sand. If you picture "Goober" from the old TV show Andy of Mayberry with a chunk of sandpaper, working on his 52 Chevy pick up truck, you can visualize him working the paper so hard with his fingers that he leaves marks everywhere instead of a smooth flat surface. If you ever sand without a pad and you feel the paper getting hot, you are working it too hard. How would I know that…..

Once I worked over all the surfaces I blew off the car and wiped everything down with a clean rag and bucket of water. Not real wet, just enough to clean all the dust off so the spot putty will stick. After letting everything dry real good, I walked around the car with the spot putty and plastic applicator. Any little pin hole gets covered. Any scratch or chip gets covered. Any low spot that shows up from sanding gets filled. You can tell a low spot by the change in color of the gray primer after sanding with sticky the stick. If it's not uniform, there is a low or high spot. High spots get worked down with the sand paper. Low Spots have to be built up. Spot putty, when applied real thin dries quickly. If you have to apply it over more than an inch in diameter area or thicker than 10 thou of an inch, then you should be using Bondo.

Be careful when sanding spot putty, it plugs up the sandpaper and will smear or chunk if you work it hard. Sand very, very easy. Turn the paper wrapped around sticky the stick or the sanding pad often and slap it against your thigh to clear it out. Ouch! Not too hard. Maybe I should slap it against my butt!

After sanding everything down, applying the spot putty and sanding all that down, it's time for round two of the primer. It works the same as round one but it's usually more difficult to see where you have painted and where you have not. If you are not careful, you can miss some spots and have some thin areas that you may sand through later. It's important to have a spray pattern strategy so you have uniform and complete coverage. One coat should be left to right and the second top to bottom. Things turned out pretty good. I did my usual leaf blower cleansing of the garage and let things set for a few days.

I decided to put the Europa project aside for a few months and finish up my 1965 S2 Elan project. I had bought the Elan a few years ago and did a complete body off including sandblasting and powder coating of the chassis. It was running well with a few things left to do and nearing completion but I just was not happy with the paint. I had used an off brand of sealer and had trouble with my compressor spitting moisture into the paint so I had some spots on the Elan that looked like wrinkles. They wouldn't sand out and they were bugging me - a lot. The Elan was painted with Enamel paint. My Seven that I had painted after the Elan was painted with base-coat/clear-coat and it had turned out terrific. So after many months of stewing I just decided the heck with it. I decided to sand down the Elan and re-paint it. I pushed the Europa chassis across the alley to my neighbor Louise's garage. Her girl friend's van didn't fit in the garage so she had an extra parking spot that she was willing to let me use. She had given me the garage door opener to her double-doored garage. One door opens up to the alley and me. The other door opens up to her driveway on the other side. I pushed the Europa chassis over and hit the remote to open the door. Unfortunately I hit the wrong button and both doors opened. No big deal except Louise's two Pit Bull puppies were playing on the other side of the driveway door. They saw me and started running towards me while I frantically tried to get the *&$#ing door to close real fast! I got it closed. I hadn't had a chance to bond with her puppies yet and I didn't want to be the first to see if they had any mean streaks in them where they would want to playfully lick my face while they ripped out my throat.

With only the ally door open I pushed in the Europa rolling chassis and parked it against the wall. My son John came home and together we put the body on top of a couple two by fours on top of the chassis. I'll keep everything over there while I work on the Elan. I'll start this Europa Euphoria article series back up in a few months. Talk to you then. zog 11/12/05

Europa Euphoria by Bob Herzog Part 9 of?

4/28/06 It's been 5 months since I worked on the Europa. I went to open my neighbor's garage and I again didn't remember which button on the 3 button garage door opener she gave me opened the ally side and which button opened the house side. So once again I was greeted by Louise's two young pit bulls. Luckily for me, I had found out over the winter that they were just two very happy, friendly 75 lb pups. Unfortunately for me, they don't get out very often so at their first glimpse of an open door to freedom they sprinted. It took about 10 minutes for my son John and I to chase them down, shoo them out of a half dozen other neighbor's yards and herd them back into their own back yard. With tails wagging 100 mph and slobber drooling out of their mouths, they accepted their return to captivity.

John and I moved the Europa body out of the way and rolled the engine/trans/chassis combo onto my trusty, rusty trailer. Some day I will have to do a restoration on my 1977 trailer. It's almost old enough for me to consider working on it. Actually the trailer gets updated every so often by people borrowing it from me. Paul Quiniff borrows the trailer often so one day at work he got tired of the ugly rusty orange paint so he blew a quick coat of school bus yellow on it. Looked pretty good for a while. A couple years ago Scott Scherwan borrowed the trailer and put his 914 Porsche on it to take it up to our track day at Blackhawk Farms Raceway. Well, he hit a big pothole coming out of a toll booth and busted a leaf spring. We had it towed back home and Scott popped for a pair of new leaf springs for the old beast. Couple weeks ago Bill Greenwald borrowed the trailer and put in all new wiring and lights. I guess he didn't like the fact that only a few of the running lights and nothing else worked. Hey, anyone else want to borrow the trailer? It could use some brakes and maybe another paint job.

So spring had sprung and I had spent the last weekend pulling my Sea-Ray boat out of the cottage garage. Had to use Vaseline on the door openings to squeeze it out – real tight fit. The piers, boatlift and Sea-Ray were now in the water so I now had an empty 1 car garage. Now a one car garage may only hold one American car or a boat if you really squeeze it in, but a one car garage becomes a two car garage if the cars are of the Lotus variety. So for my summer project (when I'm not out on the water), I now had the Europa sans body in the garage next to my regular Sunday morning driver - my 1963 Elan S1. As it turned out, the first weekend up at the cottage turned into a very rainy two days. It poured steadily from noon on Saturday until well after when I left on Sunday afternoon. No boating for me. My sons had a fishing tournament on Saturday but they dressed for the weather and didn't mind the pouring rain as they fished alongside the other 99 boats out on the Chain of lakes. What they didn't like was that they didn't catch any fish. They only fish for giant Muskies and those buggers are not easy to catch.

So anyway, I jacked up the Europa engine/trans/chassis onto a couple of milk crates, turned on some tunes and started the disassembly of mechanical bits. Even though this is the newest Lotus I have ever worked on, it is still 33 years old and that's old for mechanical bits that have never been disassembled before. One thing in my favor was that the English anti-rust program comes in the form of oil seepage. Engine oil seeps out of various engine nooks and crannies and coats the entire back half of the engine/trans/chassis assembly with an $1/8^{th}$ inch coating of black goo. The first time you take a wrench to a part, the black goo leaps off the car and finds its way to a cozy spot under your fingernails. Later on when it's clean up time, no amount of gojo and aggressive application of a scrub brush will remove all of that goo. You can get most of it out, but for days you will look like you have applied eyeliner to your fingernails. Maybe that's the secret ingredient they use for toe fungus medicine. I hate those disgusting ads and commercials for whatever that product is. Maybe it's just old Lotus oil. No virus, mold or fungus could live through a coating of old Lotus oil.

Some of the bolts came off pretty easy. Some required a little leverage. This being our Cottage, all I had was a set of small sockets and my $10 set of Chinese wrenches. I didn't remember to bring up my tool box of big ratchet wrenches and breaker bars. What I would end up doing is place the cheapie wrench on the bolt and then slip a 1 inch cheapie wrench over the small wrench to use as a breaker bar. Kind of an extension for the little wrench. Only stripped one bolt....

This is first Europa that I have stripped down to its complete nakedness. Most of the items were of the familiar Cortina/Elan style engineering. But some of the parts are unique to a Europa. As the parts started to come off and pile up next to the parts cleaner, I had to decide how far I wanted to get this weekend. It's always good to have a milestone in a project to give yourself a sense of accomplishment. My wrench trick didn't work with some of the big bolts that hold the back of the trans and I didn't have anything big enough to try and unbolt the rear axles, so I decided to see if I could yank the engine before going home for the weekend. I pulled off the 33 year old hoses and oil pressure line and starter and alternator and muffler - actually, the muffler and exhaust pipe is a newer stainless steel item. The engine/trans bolts came off pretty easily but the motor mount bolts were stubborn, requiring liquid wrench and a lot of leverage.

  It just so happened that my cherry picker (actually one that I have semi-permanently borrowed) was in the basement. Since no one else was home at the time, it took a bit of planning to push that thing up the stairs and into the garage all by myself without popping something important on my body, but I did it (get the cherry picker up the stairs that is, not pop anything important). After a little wiggle here and prying there and moving the radiator pipe out of the way, I soon had the engine out and hanging and spewing antifreeze all over the place. I plopped the engine onto the engine stand, wiped most of the muck off my hands and cracked open a cold one. Since it was still drizzling rain outside, I sat in the swing under the porch watching the clouds and rain and wind on the water for a bit - just relaxing. That's what this is all about. This restoration project stuff. It's just relaxing.

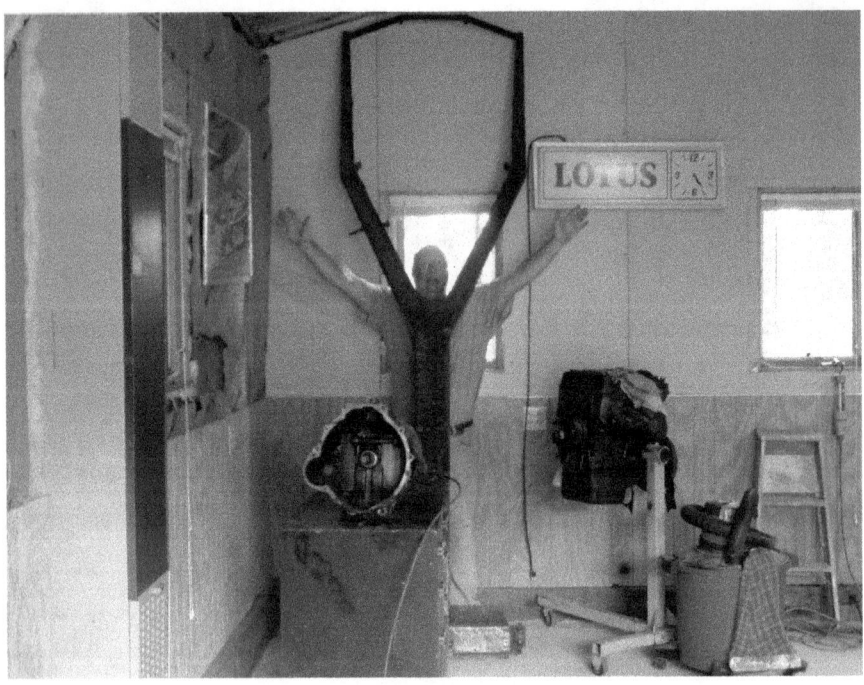

Europa Euphoria by Bob Herzog Part 10 of?

    Memorial Day weekend. We spent a good part of Saturday out on the neighbor's pontoon boat. We cruised over to a nice bar on Fox Lake and had a leisurely lunch (a little food with a lot of liquids), followed by a leisurely cruise back to the cottage. Sunday we did some movement of piers and boat lifts and some more leisurely liquid libation imbibement. By Monday I was pretty toasted from the two days of sun, external liquids and internal liquids so I planned a few hours of garaging. The first task was to remove the rear axels which require that you drive out a shear pin. These $1/8^{th}$ inch pins were petrified into place so it took quite a bit of beating with various sized drifts, ratchet wrench extensions, hammers and other weapons of mass destruction. While hammering away on the pin, I had to take care not to slip and hammer my hand that was holding the weapon locator (drift) in place. If I slipped, I think I would have flattened a finger or destroyed a knuckle. Took about 45 minutes per pin. Pretty stubborn but eventually they gave up and popped out allowing the axels to be removed. I could then take the trans out of the chassis and plop it onto an old steel milk crate for further inspection.

    A mistake I made along the disassembly way was not breaking loose the 1 ½ inch nuts holding on the rear wheel hubs before I pulled out the axels. Those are the things that hold the lug studs that you bolt the wheels to. Well, the Europa's rear hub nut is torqued down to 200 foot pounds. Quite a lot of oomph to torque it down. Quite a lot more oomph to get them off. And now that I had the axels off the trans, I had no leverage to un-torque those big nuts. I tried putting the assembly into my small table vice attached with two small bolts to my work bench which by the way bears an amazing resemblance to an old kitchen counter we used to have. As I worked on the nut with a BF wrench, all I did was move the entire work bench. By the way, the 1 ½ inch BF wrench I use to apply leverage comes courtesy of LOG 22. You remember the Lotus Owners Gathering held in Lake Geneva Wisconsin? You don't? Well go and check your back issues of Lotus Notus. Go Ahead. I'll wait…. OK, you're back? Good. So anyway, Rose & Mark Plechaty ran the show (and a great show it was) and Lotus Corps helped out. It was a Lotus LTD event so we can't technically say that it was our event, but we sure did most of the work. So anyway, Mark wanted to have something different for trophies. Something you would remember. He found some huge cheapie wrenches and had stickers made up that said LOG 22 and applied them to the wrenches. So for say first place in the show, you got a 3 foot long, 2" wrench that said "First place Elan LOG 22". Pretty cool and pretty practical as you could keep your trophies hanging in the garage and actually use them for something practical once in a while. Let's call them "trophy wrenches".

So I got 3rd place in the Elan category at LOG 22 so I got a 1 1/2 "trophy/wrench" that I was using to try and break loose those nuts. I put the axel/hub/rear link on the floor next to the work bench with a 3' monkey wrench on the axel. Next I attached the 2' long 1 ½" wrench on the nut and tried to leverage off the nut with one foot on the monkey wrench and one foot on the trophy wrench. No luck. I would push on one and lift myself up. I needed some assistance, a little extra weight. Ever play twister? I guess it could be fun with lots of liquor and loose women. Well, I had some beer and my trophy wench wife which was close enough so I decided to play a garage twister game with her to try and get these nuts off. (Ahem) Sue came out to the garage and I had her stand on the monkey wrench. I easily lifted her svelte 120 lbs off the ground with one push of my left foot. She grabbed onto the workbench to try and hold herself down but still I lifted her and the workbench. So I grabbed onto her with one arm. Grabbed the workbench with the other arm. Put one foot on the axel to try and keep it on the floor and used the other foot to push on the trophy wrench. I had one foot on the monkey wrench, the other foot on the trophy wrench and my arm around the trophy wench who was holding on to the work bench. Two wrenches, a bench and a wench! I was still lifting up the both of us with the leverage advantage so it took quite a bit of balance to put most of my road hugging weight on the axel and then just push hard enough with to other leg to finally break the nut loose. I actually had to kind of jump onto the axel at the same time I was jumping onto the trophy wrench while holding onto the workbench and onto the trophy wench who was also hanging onto the workbench. Sure seemed like more than 200 foot pounds to me. Now it's Miller time. And maybe the trophy wench will let me jump on.... Ouch – never mind!

Europa Euphoria by Bob Herzog Part 11 of?

Next trip out to the garage I was sitting on the concrete floor and unbolting things when I remembered that cold concrete kind of sucks the life out of your old body. When I would try to stand up, it would take me a couple minutes to be able to stand fully upright and move around. I have a rolling table in Des Plaines that is great for bringing big objects off the floor to a good working height. But not here up at our lake house. I looked around the basement and found an old wood chest of drawers. Seemed sturdy enough so again I called Sue out to the garage and together we lifted the greasy chassis with some remaining suspension components onto the old chest. Can't roll it around but at least it's at a working height now!

Another rainy Sunday so I spent some time in the Lake house garage. I do have basic cable TV out there though so as I was finishing up stripping bits off the chassis I got to watch Paul Tracy drive over Sebastian Boringday's head in the Champ car race at Cleveland. Also got to see the stock car boys wrestle with turning both left AND right at Sonoma. The last thing to come off the Europa chassis was the brake lines. Pretty brittle and crusty. I'm sure I will be replacing those.

I would venture to guess than every old Lotus Europa weighs about 20 lbs more than when it left the factory. There are two reasons for that. #1 is all the oil that is caked all over everything. It keeps the chassis from rusting and actually makes some of the bolts easier to break loose, but it is a mess to scrape and clean up. #2 reason for the weight gain is all the acorn shells, leaves and dried up mice mung that you find in the bowels of the chassis. I don't know how those mice get in there and make their nests, but the only way out is with my trusty old shop vac. Now since this is house number 2, we bring up all the worn out stuff up here so this shop vac is VERY tired. At least 25 years old, the motor is still quite willing; it's just everything else that is struggling. As Sue was walking through the garage, I had the shop vac going and it suddenly burped and emitted a belch of dust up into the air. The bracket that held on the air cleaner had rusted off and now all the dust in the vac was spraying all over the garage. Well, at least for 5 seconds until I could yank out the plug to shut it off. Sue laughed as she ran out of the garage to avoid the dust. Took me about 45 minutes to fabricate a bracket to hold the air filter in place. Then I spent another 45 minutes vacuuming up all the sprayed dust as well as the kitty litter I had spread around on the floor to pick up the little grease balls that had fallen off the chassis during the disassembly stage. (No Italian jokes please)

    Disassembly all done. At least everything is off the chassis. I still have to tear down and rebuild the engine, trans, steering rack, master cylinder and other bits. But technically, the tear down is done. It's Miller time! I grabbed a cold one, a lawn chair and my ledger where I have been keeping track of my hours. I added up the hours and found that it had taken me 42 hours to strip all the junk off the chassis up here at the Lake. I had previously put in 85 hours in Des Plaines taking the body off, stripping it down and getting it primed. So at 127 hours I'm turning the corner and I will now actually start the restoration work. Better have another ice cold can of planning fluid.

    Although the next logical steps at this point would be to get the chassis sandblasted and painted, that work would need to take place based out of the Des Plaines garage instead of the lake house. Since the Des Plaines garage and Des Plaines spare time was still occupied by the 1965 Elan and the final detail work on said Elan, I had to find something else to do at the lake house garage on one very, very hot Saturday afternoon. It was the day before our club picnic the next lake over at Greg and Ann Wisniewski. I decided to spend that Saturday afternoon tearing down the engine.

    I already had the engine mounted on my trusty engine stand. As I popped open the drain plug to drain the oil out, I was amazed to find so much oil in the oil pan. You would think judging by the thick coating of old oil on the entire outside of the engine that there would be nothing left inside! As the oil drained I took a chunk of scrap wood and scraped off some of the oil sludge from the outside of the oil pan letting it fall into the drain pan below. Lotsa muck all over the engine.

    As I was working in the garage, I had my big portable electric water pump running outside, sucking water out of the lake and watering the lawn through two garden hoses. It's a good size 1 ½ hp pump, so it uses all 15 amps available from the electrical outlet. In fact I can't even use the outside electrical outlet down by the water because the outlet has too small a gauge wire out there and the Romex wire heats up and pops the circuit breaker. If I run my heavy duty extension cord into the basement, the first outlet available just happens to be on the same circuit as the air conditioner. So I can't water the grass and run the central air at the same time using that breaker. All the other outlets down stairs of course are on the same circuit except for the one all the way in the back for the well and water softener. So I run the extension cord back there. Trouble with that is that when the holding tank for the house water gets low, the well pump has to run and fill it back up and pop goes the breaker. So every other time that someone flushes a toilet or turns on the TV or a vacuum cleaner or a hair dryer – pop goes the breaker. Oh, and the circuit is also hooked up to the ceiling light and fan in the garage. So at least I can tell when someone flushes the toilet and pops the breaker because the light in the garage goes out. So the routine is that when the breaker pops, I go and unplug the extension cord, reset the breaker to let the holding tank fill up. Move the hoses outside to a new watering spot. Get a beer out of the Fridge. Plug the extension cord back in. Go back to working on the engine. Repeat as necessary. I think the breaker popped maybe 6 times that afternoon. That's a lot of toilet flushes.

   I popped open the valve cover and everything looked pretty good in there. Cams in good shape, no rust, no real sludge. Cam bearings looked almost reusable. No visible wear. Hmmmmm, I'll have to see how expensive new ones really are these days. Last I heard they were becoming very rare and very expensive. The distributor, fuel pump, clutch, pressure plate and flywheel all looked ok as well. Couple of exhaust studs were broken off by the previous owner (Rich). Those will have to be drilled and easy-outed later. Popped off the head, no surprises there. Valves got a lot of gunk on them but it don't matter. Bill Truesdale at Apex will make them like new, or I'll just buy some new ones. No spare parts laying about inside the oil pan (always a good sign). Pistons popped out OK, no ridge buildup. Piston skirts in good shape and the block hone looked smooth with no real wear. Perhaps just a hone and new rings? Bill will tell me for sure.

   The only thing that was a bit askew was the timing chain tensioner. It apparently had never been adjusted so there was a ton of slack in the timing chain. The tip of the rod that pushes against the chain sprocket had nicks on it instead of a wear mark. Must have caused some performance issues.

Some neighbors stopped by for a brew just as I was pulling off the crank. They were coming in sweating from being out in the direct sun on a pontoon boat all afternoon. I was a greasy mess so I did a quick goop clean up of my hands and arms in the slop sink (excuse me, the laundry tub). I then just took off my shoes and socks and walked out into the lake for 2 minutes to cool down. I then joined them and my wife on the screened porch and dripped and drank for the rest of the afternoon. Nice way to end the day.

Europa Euphoria by Bob Herzog Part 12 of?

OK, so now it's time to take the chassis to be blasted and powder coated. I had gone up to the Lake house to replace a leaky water heater. Since I don't have garbage pick up there, I brought along my trailer to take the water heater back to Des Plaines. My ex-neighbor the plumber friend came over and helped me (actually I helped him) replace the water heater. I dragged the crusty old heater out to my trailer and strapped it down. I then went out to the garage and carried out the Europa chassis. One determined person can lift and move the chassis by oneself but it is a bit heavy and bulky. I found that if I put my 2 wheeled dolly under one end, I could pick up the other end and just drag it. I strapped the chassis on the trailer across from the water heater. After a clean up and a quick boat ride around the lake with a couple cold cans of suds, I headed back to Des Plaines. The water heater and chassis don't weigh much so the trailer did a lot of bouncing over the continuing series of bumps and pot holes that make up our wonderful Chicago-land road system. The worst roads that money can buy. And you do have to pay a lot for the privilege of driving on those crumbling lanes. I noticed that nobody tailgated me on I-294. Maybe they were smart enough to see that they might get sprayed with water or rust bits from the water heater. Or maybe grease from the chassis.

Back in Des Plaines I pulled up out front of our house and tossed the water heater out by the front curb. Now this could be a problem because in Des Plaines you need a permit to replace a water heater. So if the water heater police showed up, they could write me a ticket for not having a permit. But Des Plaines is also a culturally diverse melting pot and I suspected that someone would want the water heater for scrap metal value. Sure enough, I hadn't even yet backed the trailer under the back porch when I saw the junk truck out front leaving with my old water heater already on it. Bye-Bye.

I took a few days off the next week to relax and work on car stuff. Because I sit on my butt in front of a computer terminal all day at work, when I take a day off, I hardly sit. I took the chassis over to Astro-Blast – a big industrial sand blasting shop out near Bill Truesdale's "Apex" engine shop in Bensenville. As I unstrapped the chassis I noticed a 65/66' Mustang on a trailer along with several tons of metal bits all over the yard waiting to be blasted. They blast everything here. I had already placed old heater hose pieces over the metal heater hoses that are braised onto the chassis. Didn't want anyone bending them or blasting them away. Jose and Hose B took the chassis over to the holding area. I would pick it up in a few days.

I headed over to Paul Quiniff's shop with a station wagon load of Europa parts to be sandblasted. I had all the big suspension parts like the trailing arms, sway bar and springs/shocks, along with many, many bits and pieces. 53 parts all together. I forgot how time consuming sandblasting is. Paul has a nice big sandblasting cabinet that was donated from John Zorns' former employer. John's company was going to just throw it out. Paul was at the right place and the right time and got himself a nice blaster. Along with the 53 parts I unloaded, I unloaded 3 – 30 packs of Old Style as partial payment for letting me blast away for about 4 hours. Very satisfying work. You put a couple crusty rusty parts in the blaster, stick your arms in there and have at it. 20 minutes later you are blowing the dust off a couple of very clean old parts, ready for paint. In between parts you walk over to the fridge and grab a cold one. So you kind of get blasted while you are blasting. On a dry day with all the dry fiberglass dust (Paul says what dust?) around there tends to be quite a bit of static electricity in the air. As you are blasting away, if you stand a bit off of the blaster, every so often the static electricity will discharge through whatever body part happens to touch the blaster. Your forehead, nose, stomach and sometimes certain lower extremities of your body – yow. The other choice is to just stay plastered against the blasting cabinet so you stomach is continuously grounded, thus eliminating the zzzaaaps. But what that does do for me is it creates an electric light show. Yes, as you are staring inside the big box, working the parts through the big rubber arms, the static electricity causes you to see colors – usually green. Wow man, psychedelic! Far out!

The next day I gave the Astro Blast guy $150 bucks cash and picked up my spotless chassis. No rust holes. No rust. No paint. Just a very rough patina. From there I picked up Paul at his shop and we went down the street to his buddy that owns an industrial powder coating company. The Plastisol building covers about a square block and has assembly lines moving raw metal products through the powder coat booths and into the ovens. Business appears to be very good as he is running 3 shifts. We dropped off the chassis and a few of the larger attaching components like the trailing arms, rear cross piece and front sway-bar. Paul's buddy sends the chassis through the powder coating process during a lull in production in the early morning and he gets some spending cash ($300) from me for his efforts. Spend a little money, save a lot of work. Get great results. That's powder coating.

I've told you before, but I'll tell you again, I hate painting in my garage because it makes such a freaking mess. So I got up early one Saturday morning and set up a production spray paint line in my back yard. I had a big long table with a bunch of parts spread out all over, and two step ladders with dozens of parts hanging from bent up pieces of coat hangers. I had gone to my favorite paint supply house and picked up a gallon of red oxide primer. I mixed up a batch, dragged out the hose, put a latex glove on my left hand, put on a mask and started spraying primer in my backyard. Started at about 8:30am and went through two and a half guns worth of mixed primer. It only took 2 hours, but it's a lot of work. Pick up a hanging part by the coat hanger with the gloved left hand, holding it up, spraying up and down, twisting, spraying, twisting spraying. Hang that part back up, pick up another. Repeat 53 times for the first coat, and then paint everything again for the second coat this time using different angles and spray patterns to ensure complete coverage. Whew! Worked up a good sweat while most people in the neighborhood were just thinking about what they were going to go get at the grocery store. I threw a little paint thinner in the gun and went over and sat on the porch with a Hawaiian punch. No I don't ALLWAYS drink beer; it was after all it was only 10 am.

Europa Euphoria by Bob Herzog Part 13 of?

Paul picked up the chassis and other big bits at the powder coaters. As usual, it turned out real nice. They plug up the holes that bolts go through with some rubber plugs so when they do the powder coating, the paint doesn't get where it is not needed. It's a pain if they don't plug the holes because the powder coat paint is thick and tough. You end up drilling out the holes just to get the dried powder coated paint out.

I took the chassis up North to our Lake house because I already had enough to do in Des Plaines finishing up some items on the 1965 Elan that I was putting on ebay. I placed the Europa chassis on top of the old bedroom chest of drawers as a sort of work bench/assembly table. Worked out real good because I can place all the readied chassis parts inside the drawers, right where I will need them. Scott Sherwan came up one weekend in November to help take out the piers and boat lift. I showed him and Paul my set up and Scott, who is an avid woodworker was immediate fascinated with the bench/cabinet. It was a hand me down from a friend of a friend that we brought in when we were trying to fill up our newly acquired lake house 6 years ago. Even though the dresser was covered in a heavy coat of ugly black paint, Scot recognized the quality workmanship and started investigating the inside of the drawers and the manufacturer's sticker on the back of the cabinet. It was well built but alas, it was not something for me to take to the PBS Antique's Road show, just a good quality 1950's cabinet – no big deal. Darn.

Carl Sarro had brought his Europa axels to one of the Lotus Corps meetings for show and tell. Carl was working on some noise coming out of the back of his pristine original "TC Special". After looking at his axel splines and comparing them with mine, I could see that I had a problem with mine. What I thought were supposed to be pointy splines turned out were supposed to be square edged splines. I went back and looked at mine and then conversed with Paul who had and extra axel shaft left over from his S2 Europa project. Now both Carl and Rich had told me that the TC axels were bigger than the Renault S2 axels, but I measured them several times over and they looked to be the same. So I took the axels' apart and put together the best parts from all the pieces. I will just have to make sure there is no wiggle or jiggle when I start assembling the rear hub stuff. Yes, that's technical talk.

R.D. enterprises has monthly specials every month. (imagine that) One month he featured new rubber heater hoses. These are about 5/8 diameter but they have special bends in them so you can't just replace them with straight hose. So I had picked up a pair and those happened to be the first parts to go back onto the Europa. Finally, we are putting things back together! Couple little new hose clamps and a little tightening with the screwdriver and those things should be in place for the next 33 years of so. That's how old the original ones are. Nearly impossible to replace once the car is all back together without pulling the engine/trans, so I hope they are good forever. I took a look at my tally and found that I had spent only a total of 186 hours to get to the point where I am finally putting things back together. Not bad, but still a long way to go.

Next parts to focus on were the front arms. I had bought and installed all new bushings for the upper and lower arms but now as I offered up the parts (an English saying that Greg Zelazek is fond of) I noticed that the upper and lower shafts were of slightly different diameter. The upper shaft diameter was .502 and fit just fine through the chassis and the upper arms. The lower shaft was .507 however, just thick enough so it still fit through the chassis, but not through the new bushings. That 5 thou of an inch was enough to stop the assembly progress. But I had learned long ago that when you reach a road block in a restoration, you write down what needs to happen, put it aside and move onto something else. That something else that weekend ending up being a walk across our frozen lake with Sue and a sack-o-beers. Yes, that is one of the many things where we are quite compatible.

On our next trip up to the lake, I brought along a half inch adjustable hand reamer borrowed from Paul. If there is ever Armageddon, I am heading over to Paul's garage because he has everything you could possibly need for any situation. He's got spares for his spares. It took a while to figure out how the adjustment worked but in a few minutes I was reaming the .502 diameter bushings out to .507. Doesn't sound like much but those babies are tough. Plus, the inner race is just kind of melted into the rubber so if you are overly aggressive (who, me?) you end up with the inner race just spinning inside the rubber part and no metal gets reamed out. So you have to be pretty patient, and you have to have good strong wrists. All those years of 12 oz. curls I'm sure helped there. But in the end I did end up cheating a bit and I used my Dewalt electric drill on a real, real, slow, slow speed to gently hone out the bushings until they all fit just so! 4 bushings – 2 hours. Not ready to go into mass production at that rate. No matter – it's done. What's next?

When installing the shafts and arms, you want to lubricate all the surface areas so they continue to be moist and allow movement for years to come. Otherwise all you have is the rubber twisting and they will wear out in about 5 years or 5000 miles, which ever comes first. Axel grease is my choice of lubricant here as oil will eventually wear out and disappear.

Back in Des Plaines, I had the Europa body stored on a couple old milk crates underneath the back porch. I had it wrapped up with a couple tarps held on with bungee cords to keep the elements and critters out. As the cold winter wind blew one day I found out that Europas may be very aero-dynamic from the front, but not from the sides. As a cold front from the North came trough one night I heard a ka-whunk. (⬅= does not pass spell check) The next morning I found that the Europa had taken flight and was now partially into my neighbor's yard. At least it didn't knock the legs of the porch out on its short trip. Since it was just a bare shell, I was able to swing it back onto the crates by myself. I did some creative strapping of the bungee cords onto the milk crates so hopefully it won't take flight again. At worst it will walk itself off the concrete into the yard. I want to avoid those Ka-whunks. Those usually have to be fixed later.

Europa Euphoria by Bob Herzog Part 14 of?

Europas have these real long steel tubes that connect the fluids in the engine that's in the back to the radiator that's in the front. The tubes are 2" in diameter, about 6' long and held in place with rubber grommets, front and rear. These particular tubes were in pretty good shape on the outside but I could see a lot of white corrosion on the inside. I took some rolled up sandpaper and sanded out the gunk from the first 6 inches at each end. To get the gunk out on the other 5', I taped up one end and poured in some radiator flush. I taped the other end and shook the slush back and forth for a bit and then let it sit and soak for a couple hours. Upon my return, I opened one end and poured out the yucky sauce from within. I did one more flush and then hosed everything out with the garden hose.

I brought the tubes back into the garage and I knew that the metal guts needed to be dried quickly and then sealed up with some paint. I attached my shop vac (got a brand new Sears jobby for Christmas – woo-woo! You can even take the motor off and use it as a leaf blower – arg-arg-arg!) to one end and sucked some air through the pipe to dry things out. As I was standing there letting the air dry things out I happen to notice one of those foreign lady bugs (not the nice domestic type) crawling on one of the garage windows. I held up the tube and sucked that bug off the window - fwip. While I was there, I just decided to clean the spider webs and other dead bug bodies off the window as well. The natural progression led me to start cleaning dead bugs and debris off the floor. As I was doing this I could see out of the corner of my eye that Sue had opened up the garage side door and looked over at what I was doing. Her jaw kind of dropped a little bit and she just turned and left shaking her head. What the heck is he up to now, vacuuming up the garage with a big long tube?

OK, so now the pipe is dry and I have to apply some paint. I picked up a rattle can of rustoleum black and sprayed into the tube. Hmmmmm. I could picture in my mind the atomization taking place and the little particles trying to float their way through the tube. I decided to try and help those particles on their merry way by blowing into the tube. So now picture me spraying into the tube and then blowing into it. Next, picture Sue looking at me in puzzlement as to why I had a round black ring of black paint on my lips. I didn't get a good night kiss that night! I finished off by pouring a bit of black enamel paint into the tube and turning it around and around as it ran through to the other opening. I think I got pretty good coverage on the inside. I took a paint brush and painted the outside real good and set them off in the corner to dry for a week or so.

Time to take the engine bits to Bill Truesdale at APEX. I put the lump (another English term for the engine block), head, crank, pistons and water pump into the back of the Audi and went over to Bill's. Things still look the same. Engines, engines and more engine bits than you can imagine. Only now there is a mixture of British and Japanese engines spread out over every horizontal surface and spare inch of floor in the shop. Business is so good now that Bill and his ever faithful companion Dave (not Tonto) seem to almost have too much work. Could there really be such a thing as too much work if you own your own shop? The Japanese engines are a neat story. It seems that a few years ago some rice racer blew up his engine real good and was looking for an expert to weld some broken aluminum bits from the head back together. Bill did his usual outstanding job and now Bill is the builder of choice for all the rice racers in the Midwest. There is a whole Clan (or do they say Cran?) of rice burner racers who have Bill build them an engine. They rebuild their Mitsubishi, Toyota, Subaru or Nissan and they take the car to the chassis dyno down the street. They hook up the car to the dyno and do their racing that way. They try to out dyno each other instead of doing street racing (which I'm sure they do a lot of also). So when they over boost the turbo and massive block or head ventilation occurs, bits and chunks come a flying out of their engines. They take the pieces back to Bill and the process repeats itself. So Bill is always busy welding up holes and regrinding cranks and replacing bent valves. Good to see he is busy. I told him I was not in any hurry. He said "Good".

Back to the chassis at home. I am replacing all of the bushings of course and a couple of them are pretty stubborn to install, specifically, the sway bar bushings. You are supposed to slide the rubber bush over the bar and then push the drop link over the bush. Well, push and push I tried. I even made up some healthy washers and fixtures to try and squeeze things together with a vise and channel locks. After an hour of sweating with no results I took them over to Paul's to see what we could do with his hydraulic press. Mr.

Engineer immediately assessed the situation and made additional pressing/squeezing fixtures out of some old hardwood on his vertical mill. It then took all four of our hands to manipulate the bar and various devices into place so we could hydraulically press the drop link over the bushings. Took an hour and Paul was doing 99% of the sweating this time but we got them on without destroying them.

Next up was replacing the throw out bearing which I will tell you again that they named it a throw out bearing because every time you see one, you have to take it off and throw it out. A little gear puller action and an appropriately sized socket was all that was needed here. A 5 minute job with the right tool – really!

Finally I pressed in the new bushings for the lower control arms that go between the transmission and the hub carrier. Another 5 minute job with the right tools – amazing!

Back up in Antioch I started putting the hub carriers back together. I had to replace one of the sealed ball bearings as it was a bit noisy. Spun real freely, just made noise and you could feel things were getting kind of loose inside. The hub carriers were both sandblasted clean so the bearing and seals pushed into place with ease, but not too easy. You don't want the bearing spinning inside the hub carrier. They are made out of unobtainium.

The hubs bolt up to the big long trailing arms that pivot off the chassis. Hey, it's starting to look like something now! What, I don't know but it is something. That's progress. Time to call Sue over and go: "Look! Arg-arg-arg." She said: "Oooooooh kiss me you manly beast." Yeah right, she went back to her gardening.

Europa Euphoria by Bob Herzog Part 15 of?

I took a few months off working on the Europa to finish up assembling Paul's Elan. (Let me refresh your memory on the history of this car.) A psychedelic Flashback to 1996 if you will.... This was the blue Sunday morning cruising Elan that Paul was almost squished in while sitting in line at a tollbooth on the way back from a pleasant day of watching a race at Blackhawk farms. Paul had noticed a Ford truck approaching from behind with no intention of stopping so he turned the steering wheel to the right and readied himself for impact. The truck slammed hard into the back of the Elan, its bumper plowing easily through the fiberglass and stopping forward progress after impacting the roll hoop. Since Paul had the steering wheel turned, the impact caused the Elan to squirt off to the right through a hole in traffic. The truck continued forward and hit the next car in line hard enough to actually break the front seats of that car off their runners! Luckily Paul's head is mostly concrete so when the bumper pushed the roll hoop into his head, he only needed a dozen stitches. The car was a total loss, basically flattened in the back but it could have been much worse. Next time you are in his Fiberglass shop, ask to see the old gas tank. It is pretty flat from the truck tire running over it!

So anyway, Paul had bought the car back from the insurance company after they settled things. Paul had spent lots of time over the years doing the majority of the restoration, straightening out the chassis, reinforcing it with steel tubes, glassing on a new back half of an Elan onto the old body, having the car re-painted and doing most of the mechanical restoration. But then Paul got busy with other projects and this Elan just sat for 3 years. He asked me to help finish it up for him and I did. 7 months/194 hours later and voila! Paul's got his Sunday morning ride back. I don't think he will be taking it back to Blackhawk however....

So Paul's got his Elan back and I now had an open parking space in my garage. I cleaned things up and pushed my big rolling cart out to porch to retrieve the Europa body that had spent most of the winter actively blowing off the milk crates it had been sitting on. We were now also in the middle of the unique Midwest experience called the 17 year Cicadas. I pulled off tarp number one of two and found about 50 of these big buggers. Most of them looked to be dead but some of them started crawling around. I don't know if they thought they were going to sleep there for the next 17 years or if they just crawled in there to die. Whatever, they got shaken out of the tarps and into the lawn. The Cicadas are kind of creepy but quite harmless. They make quite a symphonic noise when they are in full bloom, like a train rolling through town. They make quite a noise when you step on them as well. Crunch!

    My older Son Mike came home from his new job and helped me pick the Europa body off the crates and place it on the cart which we then moved out into the alley for some leaf blower and garden hose cleansing action. Mike is home now, done with College. He graduated in 4 years from Northern Illinois University with a Mechanical Engineering degree. He landed himself a nice Mechanical Engineering job with full bennies and a nice paycheck. He bought himself a new car (with a little help from a graduation gift from us) - 2007 Saturn Aura with the 255 hp Caddy engine and paddle shifters! He's got the car payments to go with the car as well. He's engaged to be married to his High School sweetheart – Wow, how time flies! I remember when he used to ride his bike under this porch. Now, at 6'5", he has to stoop quite a bit just to get under the porch without a bike!

    My first activity once the Europa settled into its new spot in the garage was to do a quick 220 grit sand job on the previously primed surface. This was to take down some of the dirt that had accumulated over the winter and to identify any chips, scratches, shrunken spots or missed non-perfect spots. Things looked pretty good. There were a couple little spots down low where the body had impacted the ground during one of its winter flights from its perch on the milk crates out into the back yard. There were a couple little chips on some edges that would need a little Bondo. I found a tear in the fiberglass under the nose at the top of the front opening. It must have happened when we picked up the body and originally moved it into my neighbor's garage across the alley. I drilled a hole into the end of the tear to take out the stress, ground down the top and bottom of the tear and did a little fiberglass patchwork. A little follow up with some Bondo would make everything look just fine.

    After some further reflection I decided to spend a little more time making the doors and hood fit a little better than stock. Some of the shows you see on DISH TV revolve around some famous car restoration shops and how they restore a jalopy into a show car in just a few weeks. They cut corners by using gallons of Bondo, something I won't do, but their technique when applied sparingly is OK. To make the seam gaps just right they basically smear Bondo across the entire gap between the door and its opening and then cut the door back out with a knife or hacksaw. They then build up and sand off things until they have a perfect gap and smooth line. The thing that applies to fiberglass bodies is that the old Europa and Elan bodies warp over time, so when you align on one corner of a door, another corner sticks out or is recessed. It's always a compromise to align things. But with a little bit-o-Bondo, you can make the Europa gaps and edges look like they came out of Japan (or at least Detroit!) I've got a pretty good feel for the Bondo thing. Not quite like a pro as it does take me a couple of applications to get things the way I want them. I duct taped the edge around the opening of the hood, put the hood back in the opening and applied a bit of Bondo over the edges of the hood that were a bit low and slopped it over the gap to the body. As the Bondo began to set up I took a hack saw blade (Hey, is that Herzog the hack holding a hack saw!) and hacked or sawed open the gap between the hood and the duct tape. I popped off the hood and let things set up a bit before sanding things down. I popped the hood back in the hole and repeated the Bondo process. After sanding I applied a coat of gray primer. I then used the foot long big block hand sander to find the high and low spots. One more real thin coat of Bondo in some spots and then it's sanding time again. Another coat of primer and things are getting real close. Once more with the big sander and then it's spot putty time. Just a little dab applied here and there followed by a little 220 grit sanding and a final coat of primer. This time it's 400 grit sanding outside in the sunshine so I could really see if there are any sand marks or pits that need a little more work. Everything looked good so after one more coat of primer, I let things cook in the sun and then put the hood back on the car. About 8 hours total to get the hood just right. I'm not quite ready to work in a body shop but who's in a hurry?

Europa Euphoria by Bob Herzog Part 16 of?

Back up at the lake, chassis assembly was moving along. Front uprights and shocks went on without a hitch, but the front sway bar was a chore. The front bar is mounted to the bottom of the front shocks with rubber isolator bushings. However, the bar normally sits flat when the car is sitting flat on the ground. Up on the stand with the front suspension in full droop, the mounting points of the two shocks are actually too close together. So I had to get a tie down from one of the wave runners and cinch the ends of the bar together, actually deforming the bar enough to mount it. Once I had it all bolted up I released the tie down and everything went – boink! But it all stayed where it was supposed to and so it was on to the next task.

I spent a good afternoon figuring out how the rear hubs mount to the big trailing arms. The pictures in the book are deceiving and they actually mount backwards from the way I interpret the drawings. This particular Europa has the very rare Rich Cwik rear disc brake option. Actually Honda Prelude brakes because that is what Paul Quiniff had put on his tube frame Europa. Rich's special brackets had 8 different possible ways of being mounted, but only one way was correct. Of course I tried all the wrong ways first.... Finally I just decided to go back to a stock drum brake set up. I just didn't like the disc brake set up. I don't think it would have lasted very long. Rich said he would go through is supplies out in Princeton and get me a set of original drums.

I put the steering rack back together all cleaned up and full of new grease. It went back onto the chassis with relative ease. I just had to figure out how to get my big hands inside the chassis to fish the bolts through. It's one of those deals where sometime later you notice you are dripping blood all over your nice clean frame and you wonder how that happened....

Front suspension went on real easy. Rich had installed new parts including Triumph TR6 brakes which are a bit bigger than stock. Just needed a little cleaning here and there. I took the D/A sander to the discs to take the surface rust off. Cleaned and re-packed the wheel bearings and torqued everything down. No problemo!

I had to spend a bunch of time looking at drawings in the factory shop and parts manuals to try and figure out what cables go where. Some are supposed to go through the chassis tunnel; some get routed on the outside. (But inside the body of course) The brake lines were the first thing I had to figure out. The T/C Europa normally comes with a pair of brake boosters in the rear of the car. Since the master cylinder is in the front, this necessitates running brake lines from the front to the rear and back to the front again. Many negative phrases have been written and much cursing has taken place over the years relating to bleeding the brakes and/or keeping the brake boosters boosting properly. Rich had removed the boosters in this car so I decided to just run the lines I needed and not try to find and restore brake boosters of questionable return for my frustrations. I had bought a rebuilt master cylinder on ebay, one that had a smaller bore so the pedal pressure required to apply the brakes would be reasonable. If you just remove the boosters and don't change the master cylinder to a smaller bore size, you need King Kong legs to stop the car. Not a problem for me but I intend to sell the car and the prospective buyer may have English sized calves instead of super sized tree trunks like mine.

After cleaning up and installing the brake lines I removed the master cylinder and put it away as eventually when It's time to plop the body back on, the master cylinder is in the way and has to be off the car. Same thing goes for the steering column shaft. I made sure the knuckle fit over the splines of the steering rack input shaft but then removed it for installation after the application of the body.

I started bugging Bill Truesdale at APEX about my engine bits and in a couple weeks he had it all ready. The head had needed a bit of work; all new valves, valve guides and a valve job. Valve seats were fine. He sent out the head to a shop that specialized in removing broken studs as this head had two busted studs to remove (I didn't do it!). The shop does sort of a reverse welding called EMD? It discharges the unwanted metal without harming the soft aluminum head – cool or actually, I imagine it was quite HOT! Block and crank were fine. Polished up the crank and did a dingle ball hone on the block after a nice hot tank to remove the usual rust in the water jackets. Main bearings, rod bearings and rings were all standard! Rebuilt the connecting rods both big and small end. Shot peened the pistons so they looked like new. Took a surface cut to the head and block to make sure they were perfect. Water pump was so rotted that he had to replace all the guts plus the inner ring. New freeze plugs and jackshaft bearings finished up what I needed. $1,000 bucks ain't bad for all of that.

I took all the goodies up to the lake for assembly there. First step was to re-clean everything with brake clean and paint the block and oil pan. I found some New Ford Gray that looks like a stock Lotus color. Taped everything up and now my old tree stump out back now has a gray outline of an engine block and oil pan on it. Fresh paint always gives you a nice sense of accomplishment. I'm referring to of course fresh paint on the block & pan, not the tree stump...

I've got a special engine stand mount that bolts onto the side of the block where the motor mount goes. Makes for an easy assembly as you can install everything including the flywheel and clutch with ease. I guess I could also mount up the trans when I'm ready but I don't know if I would trust just those 4 measly little bolts to hold everything, especially since it would be in shear tension. Maybe I'll support everything with the cherry picker. I'll think about it later.

On an Elan restoration, I usually wait till I've got absolutely everything else done before I build the engine. You don't want the engine sitting there together staring at you and saying "start me, start me". Once you get the car started, you are more motivated to drive the car than you are to finish up all the little details like interior bits. But with this Europa project, I wanted to have the rolling chassis with engine and trans in it all ready when I plopped the body back on. So I put the engine back together. It went real easy. Actually quite satisfying as all the pieces went back together all neat and clean. I had sandblasted the valve cover and now it got a good coat of black paint. I then sanded off the top layer where the fins stick up so it looks real cool. As I was checking things out I noticed there was no input shaft bushing in the crank. Strange I thought. I don't remember pulling it out. Bill must have done that I thought. So I couldn't put on the flywheel, clutch and pressure plate until that was done. That kind of killed the weekend as I had to wait till Monday to call Ray at RD Enterprises to order up a new bearing. I called Ray and he asked "You want the kind that mounts in the flywheel – right?" Uh.... I guess I didn't know that's where it goes. So I had to wait till the next weekend to go back up North and find out that yes,

I did already have an input bearing in the flywheel. Unfortunately I also found out it was shot and had to wait again till Monday to then order that one from Ray. Oh well.

Europa Euphoria by Bob Herzog Part 17 of?

I got the engine all buttoned up and looking very pretty sitting on the engine stand. Now it's tranny time. Got her all cleaned up and spiffied up with a fresh coat of silver paint during a previous visit, time for some mating action. Mating the engine to the trans that is. What were you thinking? I dragged the cherry picker up out of the basement (so a cherry picker is used in the mating process eh?) and used a couple tie down straps to hook around the transmission. I then positioned a milk crate so that it supported the trans kind of close to the height I wanted. I then started the engine/transmission mating ritual which starts out with a little lubrication – on the pilot bearing and the shaft. I then lined everything up and began the insertion. I engaged the shaft into the pressure plate opening but it would not fully find its way all the way in. Seemed like a real tight fit (something I'm not used to) so I assumed a position that gave me a Déjà vu feeling (from that very morning in fact). I was behind the trans, reaching around to the engine and kind of just grabbing and pulling everything toward me. The difference between this and the morning routine is that I will have bruises on my legs tomorrow as a result of this engine/trans mating ritual. Months later I will have bruises on my head as a result of Sue reading this chapter.

As I grabbed onto the engine I thrusted myself forward with the trans, trying to press the input shaft of the trans past the pressure plate and all the way home into the pilot bearing. I could feel and see that everything was going in only so far. The pilot shaft seemed to be getting past the opening of the pressure plate and to the splines of the clutch, but it was either hanging up on the splines or the pilot bearing. Since I had already checked that the bearing was indeed the correct size, I took off the pressure plate and clutch and re-verified that everything was lined up via a spare shaft. What I probably should have done now thinking back was to see if the trans would hook up without the clutch and pressure plate thus verifying that the input bearing size was ok. Too late now. What I ended up doing was getting everything in as far as it would go and then drawing everything up the last ½ inch with long bolts. No funny noises or clicks so I thought it was just a real tight fit. I've got it all bolted back up fine now.

Next step was to put the engine/transmission into the chassis. This is done from underneath so I had to get the assembly up to the chassis which was up on the assembly dresser. To do that, I lifted the eng/trans up with the cherry picker and gently dropped it onto my trusty rusty little red wagon. This is the wagon I had bought for $6 at a garage sale about 25 years ago. It was beat up and tired then, it's much worse now. The wheels are worn and really wobbly now. I have big washers on the axels to try and keep the wheels from falling off because the holes are so worn. But it still works. So I plopped the eng/trans down onto a couple of big towels in the wagon bed to protect the paint on the oil pan and placed a tie down strap around the whole thing to keep it in place. I then had my able assistant assist me in the location of the engine/trans. She wheeled it into place as I stood ready in a wide stance with big gloves to try and catch everything should the wagon decide to give it up and collapse. Right! A lot of good I would be. It didn't collapse and Sue wheeled it into position. Now that it was all in place, Sue could go on with her normal boring life and I would continue with the assembly. That's OK Dear; you can thank me later for this thrilling part of your day – right!

   I strapped the eng/trans to the cherry picker and slowly raised it into place. Lots of moving this way and that to get it into position; once raised, I bolted on the large triangular plates that go between the motor mounts on the chassis and the engine itself. Took only a few minutes to get three out of four of the final motor mount bolts hooked up. That last bolt as usual took almost an hour. No matter which way I twisted, tugged, pried, raised, lowered and cursed at the engine, I couldn't get that last bolt to line up and go in. Finally, after a trip to the washroom and a little more prying with a small crow bar – it went in! That was it for that weekend. I hung the back end of the trans on a little ladder for support and it was Miller Time!

Europa Euphoria by Bob Herzog Part 18 of ?

Back in Des Plaines, it was time for some paint on the body. I had spent a day shooting the final shots of primer and sanding it all down with 400 grit. I blasted out the garage with the leaf blower and headed over to Portage paint in the city. Traffic was a mess and when I got there they were having trouble with their mixing machine, not a good thing when you are spending $250 on a gallon of red paint. You heard me right (or at least you read me right) $250 for just the gallon of red paint. Another $60 for the two gallons of reactive reducer and $120 for the clear coat. I had stopped at the bank on the way and had withdrawn $600 thinking I would have some spending cash when I was done – well har-de-har-har! The total ended up to be $580! And I didn't even get fries with that! Nor a massage with a happy ending! Oh well, what are you going to do? It's the cost of doing business if you want quality paint. I had done some research on the internet and found places where you can get a paint kit to paint your whole car for about $200. But they only have generic colors and I would imagine that just like an Earl Sheib paint job, the paint would be fading in about a year.

So I got the two boxes of paint stuff home and prepared myself for a long day of painting. I finished washing the main body and body parts with clean water and took a mop to the garage floor. That was enough for one day (14 hours in the garage) time to start fresh in the morning.

The next morning I did another wipe down of the body and body parts (car body, not my body) and took things out of the garage that I didn't want painted red from the over-spray. Things like bicycles, clean towels and the other cars. At this point I have done enough paint jobs in the garage that I'm not real picky about moving stuff or covering stuff. Everything is dirty anyway so why bother. The next garage will remain sterile. I may even find some time someday to do a garage restoration!

I tacked everything off with the tack rag, mixed my first batch of red and donned my human fly gas mask. I had propped an old box fan under the single garage door and opened a screened window to get a little air flow. I had learned the hard way that you need to get rid of that paint cloud. If you don't you can't see anything! The first coat went on fine, moving about the garage bending twisting, stooping, kneeling, getting up on milk crates and sometimes actually standing up straight as I sprayed away. When the gun would sputter I'd stop and mix up another batch. I waited about 30 minutes and started coat number 2. No problem there and so after about an hour I was all done, cleaning out the gun and going outside to dry off my sweaty forehead and get some fresh air. Even though you have a good mask, you can still smell the paint and your breathing is a bit constricted. You always have to blow your nose when you are done and then check the Kleenex to see how much paint got through – ewwww, red boogars!

The red looked good with coverage everywhere (on the car body, not on the Kleenex) so I tacked everything down and started the same prep process with the clear coat. The clear shoots a lot different than the color; kind of like enamel in thickness but it does run if you are not careful. I tried to not overdo it because I have had problems with runs and curtains before on previous paint jobs. You spray the clear on too thick and everything looks good and an hour later it starts to run! The problem with being conservative in shooting clear is that you end up with orange peel or too thin a coat of clear coat. The pros do it enough that they know how much is just enough. Amateurs like me spend a lot of time with sandpaper later. And I have lots of 600, 1200 and 2000 grit so I am ready! So as I'm shooting the second coat of clear I had to be extra careful that I didn't lean onto a painted part to reach another area. The inside of the front trunk was a little tricky to get at because of the height I had the body at. So as I was up on the milk crate I tried to support myself with one hand on the ceiling and then lean over to get the inside edges real good. Unfortunately, by just holding the ceiling I disturbed the dust and some major boogars floated down into the clear on the nose (the car body nose, not my nose). Oh well, everything comes out with a little wet sanding and a rub-a-dub-dub.

Europa Euphoria by Bob Herzog Part 19 of ?

After doing some research (talking to Carl Sarro and Rich Cwik), I found out that the color of the wheels was not really truly straight black. They are supposed to be a little bit more of a real dark gun metal color. My wheels were all sandblasted clean so I went and got the spare out of the attic to have a look at the original color. Sure enough, not quite black (kind of like Tiger Woods, Louis Hamilton and Barack Obama black?). After doing some analytical reflection (a couple of beers) and noticing that I had a quart of black enamel on the shelf, I decided that straight black was good enough. So one sunny afternoon I put the wheels out on a table in the back yard and painted them with black enamel. As I was mixing what little black paint I had left I also found I had even less hardener left. I took a little enamel reducer and swished it around in the hardener can and got every last drop I could out of it. It's just that a one pint can of hardener costs about $30, and I don't want to buy another if I don't need it.

A couple days later I got the d/a sander out and sanded off the black on the parts of the wheels I wanted to remain shiny aluminum colored. Unfortunately it was night time and rainy out so it made quite a mess in the garage. Enough that I had to get the leaf blower out again and blow out the whole garage. Next chance I got I moved the cars and bikes out of the garage and shot some clear coat on the wheels – they turned out pretty nice.

I had pulled a marathon up at the lake, working many hours on the Europa chassis to get everything all set up to travel back to Des Plaines to mate with the finished body. On a Friday in early November 07, I finished up bolting in the engine and trans. The chassis was still up on top of the dresser with the rear end supported by the cherry picker and a small step ladder. Now how do I get this down to the ground WITHOUT dropping it? After a couple of thinking suds, I got my big A-frame ladder out and a come-a-long. I straddled the front end of the chassis with the ladder, stuck an aluminum bar across the middle of it and hung the come-a-long down and around the frame. I lifted the back end of the chassis/engine/trans up with the cherry picker and picked up the much lighter front end with the come-a-long. Once clear of the dresser, I pulled that out and then slowly lowered the chassis to the ground. I didn't drop it - Whew! I drove my Elan out of the garage and drove it down the hill, through the double doors and into it's hibernation area – the lake house basement. Next up I pushed my freshly restored 30-year old trailer into the garage and winched the Europa chassis/engine/trans onto it and tied everything down. That's enough for a Friday. I grabbed a couple cold ones and walked out onto the pier to enjoy the peaceful solace of the early fall evening falling onto an empty lake. Empty of boats, but still busy with geese, ducks and a couple swans moving about. I relaxed as I planed out the next couple days. Saturday would be spent pulling out the boat, cleaning it and squeezing it into the garage. Sunday would be "take out the piers and boat lift" day. Monday would be "boy my back sure is sore" day.

Europa Euphoria by Bob Herzog Part 20 of?

I had to spend way too many hours sanding and rubbing out the Europa body. But until I was happy, I had to keep rubbing and sanding and rubbing and sanding. It wasn't that the paint was bad. It just wasn't good enough and I wanted it better. Maybe my problem is that I spend too much time watching the Barrett-Jackson auctions on the Speed channel. Sue and I actually went to the Scottsdale Arizona Barrett-Jackson auction in January of 2007. Lots of very nice cars and lots of ridiculously nice cars. We had a great time and I DID NOT buy anything!

So when I look at my pretty good paint job, I see flaws. Maybe only flaws that 99.9% of the population would not see, but I see them. Uneven orange peel can be cured with some fine sandpaper and rubbing compound, but then you are kind of sucked into doing the whole car. If you sand one area flat, you have to sand it all. In doing so, I had rubbed through the clear on a couple spots and had to re-shoot some areas. That's the unfortunate part of being an amateur. You either have to compromise on what is acceptable or spend a lot of time re-doing things till you get them right. It's important to walk away from things when you get frustrated. Having patience is tough when you have to redo things several times over. If you are impatient, you end up mucking things up again and then your frustrations double and you get pissed off and start thinking of either paying someone to re-paint the car or you start thinking about taking a sledgehammer or a cutting torch to the whole blasted thing! Can you tell I was frustrated?

In one of his wonderful monthly articles in Road and Track, Peter Egan had recently mentioned a book called "Zen and the Art of Motorcycle Maintenance". I picked up a copy of the book at the library and found it a very challenging read. The book was written on several different levels which was cool and I could handle that part. The main story line was a father and son on a cross country motorcycle trip interspersed with descriptions of maintenance and repair of the motorcycle as they crossed the country. But the real beauty of the book was the very deep philosophical debating in the author's head referencing ancient Greek philosophers along with flash backs to the main character's bout with insanity that was a result of more deep philosophical debates within his head! Whew! This Zen book as is turns out was a lot like much of Peter Egan's writings where I found a correlation between what was going on in the book and what was going on in my garage. Often Peter will discuss a topic in his monthly column that correlates to a recent or current experience of mine. I really enjoy his articles. It's the first thing I read when I get my monthly issue of Road & Track. Sometimes it's the only thing I actually read. I really don't care about the zero to sixty time of a car I will never drive.

So anyway, on three different levels the "Zen" book started talking about "Stuckness", a situation where you get stuck and are not sure what to do to get unstuck. Not glue stuck but situational stuck. In the story, the characters were kind of lost in the wilderness not knowing where to go while the philosopher in his head couldn't get around a debate in his mind regarding the term "Quality", and the main character was also having a tough time dealing with his son who was acting just like a younger reflection of himself - weird. A tough but very enveloping read. The book walked through different ways of getting unstuck, again correlating to what I was dealing with in the garage. One method of getting unstuck is just to stare at the item causing the stuckness and to let your mind work out a path. This I often do. Often this involves some Unstuckness fluids in a can. The fluids help the mind relax and find new paths. Of course the fluids also cause you to make a path to the bathroom; usually the standard path is taken there.

My wife Sue often catches me staring at a part in the garage. She thinks I'm crazy (she's right) but by staring at a part, the engin-nerd in me comes out and I figure out how the part was designed to work and ultimately how to either repair or install the part.

Another method to becoming unstuck is to bring in outside influences such as calling on other experts. This I often do as I will call upon Paul to come on down the alley, share a can or two of Unstuckness fluid and help me with an issue of Stuckness.

Outside influences can include reading the manual (oh no!) or these days can also involve research on the internet. Something Pirsig, the Zen author didn't have when he started on his book in 1968.

Another Unstuckness method is to just walk away for a while to refresh your outlook on things.

All these methods are good in that they draw you away from immediate frustrations which can lead to rash decisions. Something you don't want to do and regret later. I've seen folks get frustrated quickly and sell their car rather than deal with a "Stuckness" issue like a blown up engine that you just spent several thousands of dollars to build. Hello Phil!

So after finishing up Zen and working on my own Stuckness I finally got the Europa body paint to where I was satisfied. I then finished up a few loose ends on the chassis to prepare it for the mating with the body. The heater and radiator hoses had to be connected up in the tiny area in front of the engine. A very small area that becomes very cramped once the body is on and you can only reach things from underneath. I buttoned them up now without so much as a drop of blood!

I decided to install the gas tanks next. They are much easier to install if you have the body jacked way up in the air and you are standing in the empty engine bay. Rich had bought new aluminum tanks and I spent some time polishing them up so that they would stand out. Not a mirror finish, but pretty nice. They went in pretty easy.

I then cut out a new jute blanket to cover the chassis and act as insulation. Not that it keeps the chassis warm, but it acts as sound insulation and also makes for a very snug fit when you drop the body on. I also cut out and glued in a new fire wall insulation out of the material you use to insulate an engine hood. Scissor and a can of high temperature spray on glue and I was done in 30 minutes. Now we are starting to make progress!

Europa Euphoria by Bob Herzog Part 21 of?

Thanksgiving 2007. Time to drop the body onto the chassis. The chassis was in roll around mode and the Europa body was on its tall rolling cart. Two stout males can lift and manipulate the body into place but you run the risk of cracking fiberglass because there is nothing thick enough to hold onto. 4 stout human bodies are difficult to get together at one time so instead I wheeled the chassis out of the way and rolled the cart under a garage beam where I hung a come-a-long. I looked around the garage for something I could place in the engine bay to hook the come-a-long to. I first tried a real long old aluminum level but that quickly twisted once I started ratcheting the body up so I switched to a steel pipe I found in the attic. More better! At the front, I just crawled underneath, lifted the body up a bit with my back and pulled in a stack of old metal milk crates to support the front. So now I had the body suspended in the air. I rolled out the cart and rolled the chassis into place. I then placed a couple of short garbage cans on each side of the body as a safety catch in case anything decided to slip and go Ka-whump! I hate unwanted Ka-whumps.

I woke up my sleepy son John at the crack of Noon and he helped me with the lowering of the body. I would lower the back end of the body a bit with the come-a-long and then he would lift up the front end so I could remove one of the stacked milk crates. He would then drop the front onto the crates. We repeated this process until the body engaged the chassis. The jute blanket made it a snug fit and we actually had to push down on the body to get it all the way down. Hey, the holes even lined up – imagine that! John went back to sleep a little more before we left for Thanksgiving dinner at a cousins house. I popped open a pre-bird beverage and reflected on this milestone. I got out my tally sheet and added up the hours I had spent on the Europa restoration so far. 447 hours to get to this point from the first nut coming off to this point where the body is back on. Is that a lot? Is that a little? I don't know, but that's what it is and it's far from over. Maybe I should have kept track of how many cans of beer I consumed at the end of every milestone. Maybe not.

Europa Euphoria by Bob Herzog Part 22 of?

There is a great movie called "A Brilliant Mind" in which Russell Crowe plays a genius who goes a little wacko but still comes up with an award winning mathematical equation while he was in a bar chasing women. The equation had to do with his odds of "getting" a woman. The odds increased as the males in the bar left or made total fools of themselves, thus making more women available to him. This turned out to be a novel mathematical equation from which he would make his fame. Well the same kind of equation applies with a Lotus restoration when it comes to figuring out where parts and things go. It has nothing to do with us getting lucky with women. Certainly the odds of that happening decrease BECAUSE we spend so much time with our weird car hobby.

Taking apart a car is relatively easy and fun. The challenge is figuring out where all those parts in all those boxes go back on the car. Just like a puzzle, you start with the easy stuff around the edges and work your way to the tougher items and in doing so, you have less choices as to where those parts will go. Less holes to fill, less parts to plug into those holes. Works good unless you plug a part in the wrong hole.

In the game of chess, you always need to think and plan several moves ahead. As I worked on this Europa project, like any other restoration, I was always thinking several moves ahead. I would have several things in mind that I had to work on and get done in preparation to dropping the body onto the chassis. But now that the body was on, I was out of moves! I really hadn't thought of what my next steps would be. So I went up into the garage attic and dragged down a couple boxes of parts. Time to plan my next moves!

I started out by cleaning up the tail lights, polishing them and putting them on the car. Done - easy! Looks great! Then I scrubbed down the side markers and put them on. Done - easy! Looks great! Piece by piece, the parts began to disappear out of the various boxes. Choices among the various bolts and screws narrowed down too as the good ones went back on the car. I reused most of the bolts, replacing the rusty or stripped ones and used all new nyloc lock nuts and shiny new washers.

I started cleaning up the wiring harness. It was in pretty good shape. Not much grease, corrosion or muck but I still needed my can of lacquer thinner and a rag and wipedit all down. I always keep a gallon can of automotive lacquer thinner on the work bench for cleaning up stuff. I have separate good quality lacquer thinner on the shelf for when I paint stuff. You don't want the backwash from a dirty rag contaminating the lacquer thinner that you will be using to prime a part or a car. So anyway, I had picked up this particular can of paint thinner at a swap meet over the summer. It was a huge swap meet up in Wisconsin and the thinner was only $7 a gallon. I usually pay about $14 at AutoZone for weak Dupli-color cleaning thinner and about $18 for the good stuff at my paint supplier. With the weak Dupli-color stuff, you can slop a bunch on the rag and clean things with your bare hands. Your hands dry out but it's not real bad. With the good stuff, if you get it on your hands it will tell you immediately if you have any open cuts! It will also turn your skin white and burns a bit if you repeat the process. Good stuff! So as I opened this cheap-o can I found out one of the reasons it was so cheap. O-o-o-o-o-h that smell; it filled the garage and stayed there for days. Beware of the bargain!

As I cleaned off the wiring, I noted a long red wire that had been intertwined with the harness. I didn't remember what it was hooked up to but I figured I would figure it out when I placed the harness back in the car. The wires usually aim themselves at the components they want to hook up with and as you hook up some wires you cut down on the possible places where the remaining wires can connect to. This long, long red wire was just a bare wire at one end with no connector, and it got cleaned from one end of the harness to the other and when I finally did get to the tail end what did I find? An alligator clip! Obviously not a permanent thing, at least I hope not. I was cleaning the last part of the harness, a black, rubber sheathed set of three heavy wires when Paul stopped in to chat. He looked at the wire and asked: why are you cleaning up an extension cord? Sure enough, between the fumes and the cleaning beverages, I wasn't paying attention and I was cleaning an extension cord that was somehow now a part of the wiring harness. A previous owner had needed some wire to patch around something I guess. I guess I'll have to figure out what that was used for as well. Hope it was not meant to be permanent either. Maybe it's a real early version of an electric car. You just plug it in and go. Just not very far with that short extension cord.....

Christmas vacation week, 2007 - time to spend a whole week in the garage in between family get togethers. I decided I wanted to re-veneer the dashboard and found that I had enough wood veneer left up in the attic from the last dashboard project. I stripped off the flaky, polyurethane coated, wood veneer and power sanded down the old wood dash. I trimmed the new wood veneer to a little bit bigger than the dash, pulled off the backing and glued it in place. Now since winter was upon us, I needed to find a nice flat warm surface that I could place the dash on overnight with some large weights to compress the dash and the veneer together. Since Sue was not home at the time, I found this large, flat, warm surface being the folding table in the laundry room. Sue was in a good mood when she came home later. (It's amazing how a new pair of shoes can make a woman so happy, at least temporarily.) She didn't blow up real bad when she found that I had borrowed a part of "her" laundry room.

The next day I quickly removed the dash from "her" laundry room and trimmed out all the openings and edges of the dash; turned out pretty good. It only had a little lump where the wood veneer had a twist while it was stored in the garage attic for 20 years. I then started the process of applying multiple coats of clear polyurethane on the dash. I would apply a coat, let it dry in the garage all day and then sneak it into the computer room in the house to dry over night. The next morning I'd take it back out to the garage, block sand it down with 400-grit and apply another coat and repeat. The wood veneer was a little lumpy because of age so I put about 5 coats on before I cut out the little vinyl lettering that original Europa dashboards have so you know which switch does what. This is much nicer than the original Lotus Elans with no labels where you flipped a switch and had to listen and look around to figure out what the switch did. If in flipping the switch you heard noise than you narrowed it down to either the heater fan, the radiator fan, windshield wipers or a fire starting. For at least one of the switches you did have another clue in that two tiny little wiper blades would usually begin flopping around on the windshield. If the switch flipping didn't invoke any noise it could be headlights or interior lights you just attempted to wake up. If any of the switch flipping caused smoke or fire to appear then you knew that was the excitement switch!

I scoured the usual Lotus parts supplier in the USA but could not find a new crash-pad anywhere. A crash-pad is the vinyl covered pad that sits on top of the dash. The original one that came in this car was toast. Actually, toast would have been an improvement of what was left of the original crash-pad. There was a bit of very brittle dried up vinyl but it was mostly the orange crinkly foam that I had pulled out a couple years ago. In doing research on the net, I found a company in England called Banks Europa that supposedly made a real nice crash pad kit. A phone call later and I had one of their kits on the way across the pond. Unfortunately the exchange rate was at an all time high and the only way to ship this thing was UPS. Ended up to be 95 pounds just for shipping! So the crash pad kit and a headliner cost me $450 – yow.

The crash-pad arrived and initially looked pretty good. Nice solid fiberglass shell in a perfect shape to fit over the dash. Nice double stitched, sewn rolled edge along the front to follow the front curve across from end to end. Unfortunately as I trimmed the fiberglass to fit perfectly I found that the vent openings were ½ inch off from where they needed to be. I measured things over and over and it appeared that my car vents were in the right place, equidistant from center, but the crash-pad vent openings were offset to one side. So I had to spend a couple hours with the grinder, some fiberglass and Bondo to move the holes to where they needed to be. I then took the crash-pad and vinyl over to my upholstery guy to do the gluing. I wanted it done right and the compound curves caused visions of glue gone awry in my head. A man's got to know his limitations!

Back to figuring out where all the parts go, I again went back to the method learned from the movie *A Brilliant Mind* in that I continued with the easy stuff, whittling down what was left to figure out. Often I would refer to the service manual or parts book for a clue. Once in a while I would have to consult an on-line repository of Europa knowledge called Europa Knowledge base. I do a lot of staring at the parts. Some things are easy; some take a lot to figure out. Sometimes I wish the parts would just fly on the car from me staring at them. Where is Samantha from "Bewitched" when you need her?

Europa Euphoria by Bob Herzog Part 23 of?

I got the crash pad back from my interior guy Ken. As usual, he did a terrific job. He ended up not using the sewed in seam that came with the kit. He instead sewed his own using the extra material and as I said – it turned out great. Much better than stock but not goofy looking like a custom car interior – no dingle balls. It looks stock, just nicer than stock. I spent a couple hours fitting it, trimming out the excess and making sure the dash lined up. I had already installed all the switches and gauges into the dash so now it was time to tackle the wiring. I taped some rags over the face of the dash to avoid scratches on the install process. I then placed the dash in place and tied it in place with some string. Just kind of hanging out so I could see what was in there and get my hands in to plug in all the wires.

The wiring harness was the pretty standard British codes; B = Black, R = Red, W = White, U = Blue, BR = Brown, G = Green, LG = Light Green and P = Purple. I spent about 3 hours one Friday afternoon and had it all done. Next morning however as I sipped my coffee, waiting for the warm liquid to do it's morning magic, I caught myself staring at the brand new Europa dash that was hanging on the wall in my den. I thought I liked the original dash better and I thought I would sell this one on ebay. But the more I looked at it the more I liked it and the less I liked the dash I had just re-done and had them all wired up in the Europa. The negative to the dash on the wall was that it did not have a plug for the radio hole, which meant I would have to install a radio if I used the new dash. The positive points about the dash that I had already installed in the Europa was that it did not need a radio (hole was plugged) and also that it was already installed. Well, after the half cup of coffee had flowed through and I had done some more contemplation in the shower, I went out to the garage. I turned on the lights and then took a drop light to take a close look at the dash that I had completed and installed yesterday. I really liked the finish and the color was perfect, but it wasn't a perfectly smooth finish. You could still see where the wood veneer was a little lumpy and upon further investigation I saw my final motivation. There was a big scratch on the right hand side between the panel switch and one of the gauges! Almost looked like a crack but it was just a big scratch. Somehow I had scratched the "still a bit soft" polyurethane finish during the install process. Oh well. I just jumped in and started unplugging the old dash.

In about 20 minutes I had it out and had all the gauges, switches and glove box removed. I brought out the new dash from my den and worked over the wood with some polish and wax. It had a rough finish from sitting around for 12 years. It was new old stock. After some elbow grease it turned out pretty nice. Since this was a new dash with all new wood, I had to mark and drill a bunch of tiny little holes on the back and two on the front for mounting the switches, gauges, vent levers and glove box. I used a 1/32 inch drill bit – that's small! That process took a couple hours.

I then placed the new dash in the car and started wiring things up. Since I had just unplugged everything, the re-plugging didn't take long at all until I got to the last switch (of course!). The panel lamp switch is just a turn the knob type switch but the wood dash has to be countersunk on the back so the threads of the switch stick out enough to get the chrome round nut started. Unfortunately, I hadn't noticed that the new dash was countersunk on the wrong side. No way, no how was I going to be able to grind out the backside while the dash was in place and there was no way to swap the switches around so out the new dash came and out the can of "end of day" fluids came from the garage refrigerator as well!

The next day I gently ground out the backside of the hole where the panel lamp switch mounted. It went well but unfortunately the sawdust made it's way into all of the gauges through the holes where you plug in the lights. So now I had to take all the gauges out, disassemble them and clean them out. Argh!

Europa Euphoria by Bob Herzog Part 24 of?

I finally got the new dash and new crash pad in place and screwed into place. There are several stainless steel screws that hold the wood dash in place along the front. Unlike an Elan where the dash is just bolted up to the fiberglass body, the Europa dash becomes a part of the structure. There are little metal brackets on the underside that you bolt to and there is a two piece padded metal strip that runs across the whole front of the dash. When you are done, the whole thing is actually quite rigid. The only thing that holds in the crash pad however is the two plastic blower vents. Each held in place with 4 long self tapping screws. The vents on this car had kind of curled a bit from years of baking in the sun. They reminded me of little goofy toys I used to make with my toy vacuu-form machine back in the 60's. Not real sturdy. So before I ran the long screws through the vents and through the crash pad into the top of the fiberglass, I filled the vents full of Bondo to give them a little strength. I also gave them a little spritz of special black vinyl, rattle-can paint. The wonders of a rattle can restoration. When I was all done, it finally looked real good and felt real solid. It was one of those moments where you go bring the wife into the garage and go "looky what I did" and she will say: "Ohh you are such a manly man!" Yeah right! More like "That's real nice dear".

There are lots more parts to a Europa than there are in an Elan. Lot's of little thingies that take time up lots of time staring at the factory manual and parts book to try and figure out what they are and where they fit into the scheme of things. Bit by bit I continued emptying the boxes. I took the sun faded seat belts and soaked them in a 5 gallon bucket of hot water with black Rit dye. They turned out nice but once again Sue was not pleased with the mess I had made in "her" laundry room. I call it a slop sink. She seems to think it's a laundry tub. Go figure.

One day in the garage as I pulled the car cover off the front of the Europa I heard a clink type noise. More accurately it was a "Crink" noise because it turned out to be the cheap Chinese Lotus nose badge breaking off. As I looked around on the front end I noticed that where the nose badge was supposed to be, was now only a couple screw heads sticking out. The el-cheapo nose badge that I had got off of ebay had snapped off clean. The tiny little screws may have just been soldered instead of welded. I haven't decided yet if I am just going to just glue the badge back in place or put a real nice original badge in it's place. I have one, but do I want to part with it?

Routing the parking brake cable and oil pressure line up through the chassis tunnel and up through the holes in the body was a real chore. I read lots of stories on the internet on how everyone else had had similar problems so I didn't feel too bad. But ultimately my problem was that I was trying to fit the oil line up through the wrong hole. While discussing my stuckness with Rich Cwik one evening it occurred to me that there must be another hole and sure enough, there was a hole under the dash that I had not seen and it was just a matter of cutting out the jute between the body and the chassis and fishing a coat hanger through the new found hole. More better.

I decided that although I was doing a stock restoration, I didn't want the seats redone with the stock black vinyl. Europas get real hot in the summer with the large front windshield area so when I took the seats over to K&N's, we decided to do a combination of black vinyl on the sides, but black and dark gray cloth in the center. It should look real nice. I had done a similar scheme only in red to my original Elan back in 1988. Ken pulled the old vinyl and padding off the seats and I sandblasted the frames and coated them with Rustoleum black. I was surprised to find that the Europa seat frames are made out of the same metal used on the chassis. With the vinyl and padding gone, they are still in the basic shape of the seat. Take a look at the pictures in the Lotus Corps Gallery. Not what I expected. The seat rails were very, very bad so I did some trading with Paul for some rails he had leftover from his Europa project and I spent some more time at his sandblasting cabinet, removing many years of crusty rust. His were in good shape. Mine had been quite religious in that they were very holey.

Europa Euphoria by Bob Herzog Part 25 of?

Near the end of January 08', we hit a real cold spell in the Chicagoland area just about the time I wanted to start doing some carpet and headliner gluing and rear windshield rubber installation. My garage is heated but only insulated on the walls and a lot of heat goes up through the roof and out the cracks around the big doors. So when it was only 6 degrees out, my furnace just ran and ran and ran without getting the Europa any warmer than about 60 degree. Too cold for glue to take a set, too cold for enamel paint to harden and too cold to try and push the rubber window gasket into place. It gets a little frustrating when you want to get something done and you have a certain sequence of events you have to follow but you are limited in what you can work on. Patience! Wait it out rather than do something that you will just have to redo later.

When Rich had sold me the Europa he threw in a few extras. One of them was a New Old Stock (NOS) set of carpets. I dragged the box down from the attic and noticed the shipping label was dated 1989. I opened up the box and was pleased to find a complete set of very sound and clean new black carpets. The 1 page of instructions was printed in 1981 so these things could be anywhere from 19-27 years old. No smell, no mice mung and just a little crumpled up from sitting on end for many, many years. I talked Sue into helping out here with one of her many wifely skill sets – ironing. I brought in a couple pieces at a time and she spent a lot of time with her iron and a lot of steam getting most of the wrinkles out of the black carpet set. Looking good honey! And the carpets aren't bad either!

The first carpet piece I decided to install was the large flat piece that goes behind the seats. I scoped out how the original one was glued onto the fiber board, tore the old one off and started gluing - turned out nice. I screwed it into placed and proceeded onto the next logical piece. What happened next was that whatever piece I worked on, it seemed as though I should have done a different piece first. Each piece kind of overlaps another and no matter which piece I picked, one or more of it's edges fit under another. In the end, the piece I put in first should have of course gone in last. Oh well, turned out OK, it was just the long way to do things. It's one of those deals where when you are done, you know how you should have done it and if you had to do another, it would go a lot faster – if you can remember what you did. It's tough getting old timer's disease.

Since this new dash has a hole where the radio goes, I figured I should plug the hole with a decent Stereo. I just couldn't see putting the beat up, 25 year old am/fm cassette radio back in. I did a little internet searching and confirmed my conclusions with a Crutchfield salesman and placed my order. A nice Kenwood Stereo with single cd, pair of Sony speakers and a trick little hide away antenna that I mounted in the front boot (trunk). Of course on my next trip into Best Buy I found the same stereo on sale for $20 less – argh! Since the car is all fiberglass, I don't have to worry about a metal body blocking my radio reception; therefore I was able to mount the little plastic antenna in the front boot. You can't even see it unless I point it out to you – right there. The Stereo mounted up pretty easily and I fished the speaker wires through the little tubes with the rest of the wires going out to the soon to be installed doors.

While I was figuring out what fuses to hook the radio up to, I sorted out the last few wires still dangling about under the dash. The one big red one that converts to a black with white stripe wire I finally figured out to be a kill switch that secretly mounts under the dash. After reading about this wire it appears to be just an additional point of heartburn and does not really provide any additional car theft security so I just coiled up both ends of the wire and tie wrapped it out of site. If someone else wants a REAALLLY stock restoration, they can hook it up. Same goes for the Seatbelt warning buzzers that go under each seat. Your big butt activates a switch under the seat and it buzzes while it keeps the car from starting if you don't have your seat belt hooked up. No sense in adding additional points of failure. As to the last few wires, unfortunately two big wires which I thought hooked up to the window switches turned out to be a part of the amp meter gauge. This meant that I had to reach up under the dash, unscrew the amp gauge, pull it out and splice in these wires into the already short wires going there. The wires were short because a previous owner had changed connectors when he changed to an off brand gauge. I had cut the wires again to install new connectors to fit to an original style gauge – now things were really tight. But I got it all in.

Sometimes you just need something simple to grab, install and finish in a short time when I go out to the garage in the evening. It's nice to say "I installed the Kneuten valve today". Even if the Kneuten valve is only one piece out of a thousand, it's nice to get a sense of accomplishment. So since I really didn't have any simple Kneuten valves to install, I went to bring the spare tire down from the attic and was curiously surprised to find that it seemed to still be fully inflated after 10 years of storage. An original Dunlop SP40 tire? Maybe 30 years old? Hmmmmm? After further investigation I found that it was just petrified. It was as hard as a rock but without air. It felt like a solid tire from a two wheel dolly. I don't know if it would have been hard enough to support the car without air but I won't find out. I just filled it with air and installed it in the boot. One Kneuten valve – done.

Europa Euphoria by Bob Herzog Part 26 of?

I started thinking about applying some DC volts to the Europa to see if there were any wires that had smoke in them. You know how that goes; you hook up one end of the battery cable solidly to the battery and then gently brush the other cable against the other battery post. (I always wear rubber gloves and safety glasses for this step.) If there is a BIG arc like a welder, you back off and see what you have wired wrong. If there is little or no arc, you temporarily hook up the other terminal listen for a little POP as a fuse blows. If you hear nothing you then look around the car and under the dash to see if anything is glowing or smoking. If nothing is frying you proceed onwards by flipping switches to see what works and what doesn't. If progress is good, you proceed onwards to actually turning the ignition key! That last event usually takes several days of fixing stupid wiring errors.

So since I had not yet purchased a new battery, I hiked down the alley and borrowed one of those portable jumper battery systems from Paul. Just a little dinky one, not the big one used to jump start dead cars at a used car lot (Yes, he has one of those too!). The charge indicator light on the dinky unit did not look promising but I hooked it up anyway. No arc and no smoke! But alas, no power either. Paul's jumper battery needed a jump. I plugged it into the wall and went onto some other business for a couple hours. Later on in the day I tried it again. This time there was no smoke and no big arc but the poor little battery only had enough juice to weakly tell me that the interior light switch was in the on position and the interior light worked. But the light kind of looked like the one bad eye of Arnold Swartzeneger as the Terminated Terminator in the Terminator movie as the light got dimmer and dimmer and finally went out. Hasta La Vista baby! Time to just go out and buy a new battery.

In playing with the power I noted that the ignition switch was not automatically returning to the on position from the start position. On my next trip out to the garage I got out the shop light to have a closer look. As I reached back under the dash and grasped where the wires go into the switch it all fell apart in my hands and little tiny parts and springs began tinkling down. (tinkling down is a technical term also known as Aw ****!) Onto the nice new carpet the little pieces fell. I grabbed a plastic cup and put everything in the container before they disappeared and then took out my snips and cut off the tie wraps holding the wiring up tight and out of sight (baby, everything is not alright, up tight and out of sight!). Apparently when I had put everything together, I had pinched the tie wraps too tight with my tie wrap gun and it pulled the back of the ignition switch apart – rats!

    I disassembled the steering column with the remaining ignition switch parts and brought everything out to the work bench to work on. I figured out how it all was supposed to go back together – one copper switch plate, 4 tiny little springs, a phenolic separator and one little steel ball, but I could not figure out how the return spring fit in there to make the switch return to the "On" from the "Start" position. I spent hours flipping it, squeezing it, twisting it, hooking it here and there. Nothing I tried would give me the right combination of assembly with a return spring action. Not even assembly lube (the assembly lube is taken internally by the way…. in 12 oz applications.) Another frustrating moment where you want to chuck the whole thing across the room – Patience grasshopper!

    I talked to Paul and went looking through his spare Europa stuff up in his garage attic but could not find a switch. I then talked to Bill Greenwald who did have a spare switch. Took it apart and cleaned it all up for me he did. Took my old one as a 100% trade in too. What a great guy! I put the dash back together and did my little arc of the battery routine again. This time the interior light did not come on (popped a fuse it did) but two of the 7 dash lamps came on dimly. Just the two backlight lamps for the tach and the speedo, not the ones for the amp, oil, temp gauges - strange. I went to twist the panel switch which was supposed to control all those lights and found that as I turned the switch on, the two lights that were already on went off, and the other lights would go on. I felt like music from the Twilight zone should be playing. Doo-dee-doo-doo, Doo-dee-doo-doo. It was doo-doo all right. More like welcome to the Lucas Zone! Doo-dee-doo-doo, Doo-dee-doo-doo. Welcome to "The Lucas zone", a place where Physics and Electronic theories do not apply. Time to unhook the doo-doo battery from the goofy doo-doo lights, grab a doo-doo beer and call it a doo-doo night!

Europa Euphoria by Bob Herzog Part 27 of?

I found that I had three electrical problems. The interior light would blow the fuse when I switched it on. The turn signals did not work and the third very weird one was where some of the gauge lights would go on when I hooked the battery up but they would go out and others would light when I turned on the rheostat for the lights – as I said – weird! One bite at a time I began chewing on the problems. First bite; I took out the string of lights from behind the dash and just hung them on the passenger side floor. Not an easy process. I had to pull the radio first and sacrifice a good bit of skin from my hands but I finally fished them out. I still had the weird problem but at least by seeing them there by themselves I could eliminate any wires up under the dash shorting or crossing out one of them causing the grief. I spent an hour with the volt/ohm meter checking grounds, power input and power output. I got real good at judging how big an arc off the battery I could draw before popping one of the fuses. A little arc was OK. A somewhat large arc and you could actually hear the little TINK noise as the fuse under the dash blew. The first fuse I blew here was an original Lucas fuse. There were several more non Lucas sacrificial fuses that gave their very short lives to the pursuit of solving the Lucas electrical mysteries. I finally traced one problem down to the purple/white and purple black leads reversed at the interior light. Apparently turning on the interior light switch would induce a direct ground to the power lead which would pop fuses. It took me a while to figure that one out because while in the process of trouble shooting the interior light popping the fuse, the light itself actually burned out. It is one of those bullet style lights that took a while to find at the local auto parts store. The stripes on those purple wires are very hard to see so that was a simple mistake. Reverse the wires, hook everything back up and now the interior light works without blowing a fuse. Swat! One bug down.

    I continued on with the volt/ohm meter but I was really stuck on this one. Seems that there was partial voltage somehow feeding into the ground plane and back feeding into those lights. After going over the wiring diagram I figured out that those lights should not be on at all unless the other light switch was on as well. Knowing that made the tracing back of the foreign voltage a little easier. I finally hit pay dirt when I found that the metal bezel face of the Amp gauge had partial voltage on it. Hmmmmm. That's not right. I pulled off the mounting bracket from the back of the dash, (again sacrificing more hand skin) which I had previously carefully wrapped in electrical tape so a stray wire would not cause an arc. (I had learned that trick the hard way on my first car – 1966 Corvair Corsa Convertible. A stray wire on that car caused many dollars to be released from my very thin High skool student wallet.) But back to this car.... I pulled the wires off the amp gauge and found that the partial voltage was coming from a partial ground which was coming from the impartial alternator. So when I unplugged the alternator, the problem went away. But this did not make sense. Ha-Ha, here I am trying to make sense out of a Lucas problem – silly me! I pulled out the amp gauge and could not see any crosses, grounds or shorts. But I could read one with my ohm meter. I pulled the wires off the gauge and got out my magnifying glass. (I use that a lot there days.) After careful examination I found that there were tiny little steel filings around one of the posts on the amp gauge that were shorting the post past the phenolic insulator to the base of the gauge! Of course, it happens everyday, how silly of me... what the heck? I don't know where the iron filings came from. Apparently there is some residual electromagnetic magnetism created around the back of an amp gauge with all the current running through it. I took and old toothbrush and brushed off the filings and then taped up the back of the gauge so no future filings could gather again. I don't know where the filings came from, probably from sitting it down on the work bench at some time. Weird for sure! Swat! Another bug gone.

Europa Euphoria by Bob Herzog Part 28 of?

Having cured my electrical woes I was anxious to turn the engine over. So I did. And it cranked real nice! So I went and pulled the plugs to crank it some more to see if I got spark and oil pressure. So I did. And it did. On both accounts. Wow! I got Oil pressure, I got spark, time for some gas. I put the lawnmower gas can in the trunk of the M3 and went to the Mobil station for a fill up. I momentarily forgot the can in the trunk when I took advantage of an opening in traffic to kick the rear end out of the Bimmer. It was almost a bummer in the Bimmer as I heard a ka-whunk in the trunk but when I opened the trunk up at the Mobil station the can was still upright and sealed. It sure let out a pshhhhh though as I popped open the breather and filled her up.

Back at the ranch I stuffed a bunch of rags around the filler neck and started pouring in the gas. About 2 gallons into the process I decided it might be a good idea to look for leaks. Sure enough, some idiot had left one of the fittings loose and there was about $1.50 worth (2 ounces) of gas on the floor. (I'm the only one working on this car by the way so I'm the idiot.) I quickly grabbed a rag and some wrenches and dove underneath the tanks to tighten the line. Well, I'm not exactly svelte so instead of saying I dove under the car, you could say I kind of flopped under it.

It's always lots of fun to work under a car that's leaking gas. You have to stretch your arms out so it's not pouring on your face and so you are not laying in a puddle of fuel Also as you tighten up the fitting the gas flow then starts finding the path from your hands to your arms to your arm pits. Luckily I had on a long sleeve sweatshirt so most of it just got soaked up at the wrists. It's still not a lovely smell to bring into the house for your wife to nag you about later. It's not High Karate, it's High Octane! So anyway, I got the fitting tightened real quick but the smell of gas was now permeating throughout the garage. But not to worry, my gas attacks were far from over.

I finished up putting about 4 gallons in the tank and made sure that the gas from one tank was flowing through the hose to the other tank; so far so good. Time to see if spark and gas combined can make zoom or boom. I like zoom but I don't like boom. I cranked the engine over a bit and from the sound I could tell there was no zoom or boom happening. I pulled a plug and it was still dry so I figured that the fuel pump was a bit dry and needed something to wet its whistle. Down the alley I went to Paul's garage to pick up an old Elmer's glue bottle that he sometimes uses to squirt gas in his Formula Ford race car to get it going. On the way back down the alley I eliminated the few drops of old gas he had in the bottle and filled it up with fresh gas back in my garage. I hooked up a hose line and squeezed a little gas down into the floats of the Strombergs and a little gas down the lines back into the fuel pump. Although I was careful, this still produced a bit more of that pungent gas aroma. Time to open the garage door even though it's only 20 degrees out. I cranked the engine over again and this time it made some noise. Not a real bad noise, just the typical out of timing noise. So I started cranking the distributor a bit and cranked it again. Bit by bit it sounded better. Ended up that somehow I was 90 degrees out of time and after a few more attempts she fired up! I had cranked the idle up on the carbs a bit so the engine ran at about 2500 rpm as I quickly dashed around the car to look for leaks and/or fires. About 20 seconds into the run the front carb started spewing gas out it's vent. I quickly shut her down and got some more rags out to soak up the gas that had puked onto my nice powder coated chassis. Turns out the powder coating was quite strong and no damage was done. I tossed all the gas soaked rags out the door but the garage still reeked. I sprayed a little simple green on the spillage and wiped things down. More sacrificial rags gave their lives here. A good way to recycle old underpants and socks.

  So now the next step was to pull off the carbs and see why #1 carb was puking gas. It's normally about a half hour process to unplug and unbolt everything. By the time I was done fixing this bug I had it down to 5 minutes! I first pulled off the float bowl and checked the float level which seemed fine. I hooked up a hose and did some blowing and it seemed to shut off the flow as it should at the right spot. After conferring with Rich Cwik I ordered a set of Grosse jet needle/seat sets from RD and they arrived a couple days later. I installed them and remounted the carbs. I started her up and the same thing happened again – puking front carb. I got out my trusty rusty Sears Penske pressure gauge; the one I got for Christmas from my parents in 1974 along with the little analyzer used for adjusting points. Hardly have the need to use either of them these days. I hooked up the gauge and found that the fuel pump was on steroids. It was putting out 5 psi when 1.5-2.5 will do. I ordered a Holly low pressure fuel regulator off ebay and it arrived a couple days later. I had a problem with the ebay item as this unit appeared to be a cheap knockoff. You could tell the casting marks were not real crisp and the threads for the fittings were all a bit tight. I guess it's better than too loose. I borrowed a pipe tap from you know who, tapped out the thread and hooked everything back up. I adjusted the pressure down and started the engine up again thinking this had to be it – nope! Still puking. Off came the carbs again. This time I focused on the front carb float assembly. I took it out and made sure it actually floated in a cup of water – OK. I next checked to make sure it shut off the flow at the prescribed height by blowing into a clean fuel line – OK. Finally I noticed that the little tang that rides the needle ball was bent at an angle instead of being straight. This was causing the float to actually walk over to the side of the bowl and hang up. Ahah! I re-bent the tang, reassembled everything and finally got her fired up and running with no gas spewage. I opened the garage door to let out the fumes and opened a cold one. The sound of success – zoom with no boom!

Europa Euphoria by Bob Herzog Part 29 of?

Next up on my list of things to do was to install the front windshield and rear window. I had previously tried to put in the rear window myself with no success and had heard that the front windshield installation was no picnic either. So I called around the club to see if anyone knew of a friendly, patient windshield guy. Rich Cwik's guy had done one before so he never returned my calls. That should have told me something. He never wanted to touch another Europa. I went to the on line yellow pages and just picked out a local shop that had some good reviews from a car guy getting glass put into his street rod. A 57 Chevy is not quite a Lotus Europa but then again it's not your every day Toyota Corolla installation either. I made an appointment for Saturday. Saturday came and I set up the windshield on a table in the garage and waited and waited and waited. I putzed around on various items but did not want to get too involved with anything. The appointment was for between 12 and 2. As 2 o'clock started approaching I called the glass place and was told the guy got hung up on a job in Oswego but was on his way. Oswego? Why did I bother with a local place if the installer was at a job 60 miles away? I waited and waited some more. This was the night for our annual Lotus Corps go-kart event so we had to be on the road by 4pm. I started scheming in my head. Who could I call to come out and car sit while the guy installed the glass? Would I be able to trust him to just shut the garage when he was done? Maybe he was real good and we could just finish it all up in 30 minutes – yeah right. Well it was all answered real quickly when Hose B showed up at 3:30 Hose B is Jose's shorter brother. He was shorter than Bill Greenwald if you can imagine that. Hose B did not speak a word of English and I think you can imagine that in today's world. That's not exactly confidence inspiring. After showing him what needed to be done and seeing the overwhelmed deer in the headlights look in his eyes he got his boss on the cell phone and we scheduled for his boss to come out and do the job himself later in the week. Paul had come by during this last minute commotion so we had a few 12 ounce cans of go-kart event preparation fluids. Team Zog, consisting of Mike, John, Sue and Bob Herzog along with Paul Quiniff won the event that night by the way, so the day was not a total loss. At least the go-kart win was Lots-O-Fun and very satisfying!

Thursday came along and again I had the garage prepped for the window installation. Again I waited and waited and waited. I was on the phone to Fox Valley to see who they recommend for windshield preparation when the windshield boss finally showed up – 3 ½ hours late. I immediately suspected this would not go well either. He left his truck running (something that really pisses me off) while I explained how everything was supposed to be installed. He started working on the back window, insisting that the locking bead would be easier to install if we installed the rubber in backwards. He was crawling around on the inside of the car while on his cell phone trying to run his business. He was struggling just to get the rubber gasket to stay in place as I taped it in place. 20 minutes into things as I was getting the heat gun out to help soften up the gasket he just turned to me and said sorry – he was turning the job down. Well thanks for nothing! I kicked him out, popped a cold one and called the glass guy that Fox Valley uses. He returned my call the next day and although he was very nice, he recognized that this job would not be a slam dunk so he just turned it down over the phone. Time for plan D? I conferred with my resource – Paul, and we decided to give it a go ourselves.

On my next trip to the garage I spent a couple hours with my heat gun trying to straighten out the plastic strip that gets cut into 4 pieces and glued around the edges of the front windshield. Every time I straightened it out however, it would begin to curl back up so I ended up taping it to a couple of long wood window trim strips I had laying about. I left it that way on the floor for a couple days to take a set. Also, this gave me time to build up patience to work on the project again.

Paul came out one evening and we plotted out the steps for the front window. The next day I began cutting the strips to size and pushing them onto the windshield. I cut the strips down to the correct size, mitering the corners with an old X-acto saw. The corner chrome pieces fit over the strips to make a somewhat nice finished corner. The next day I heated up the plastic strips with the heat gun, being very careful not to melt them and then glued the strips onto the windshield. I held everything in place over night with a lot of tape.

The next day Paul and Dennis Stahl came out to assist in getting messy. We did a trial fit of the windshield and then installed some butyl rubber around the opening using a caulk gun. We also installed a couple rubber strips to assist in holding the windshield in the right place. We plopped the windshield into place and began pushing it down. This took a while. Once we had it in place we taped off the red painted area and applied some professional windshield glue between the fiberglass and the plastic strips, again using the caulking gun. We only cut a tiny hole in the tip of the caulk tube so we could get it up under the plastic strip. This required so much effort to squeeze that I soon ran out of squeezing muscle. Luckily Paul has extraordinary GI Joe, Kung Foo Grip and was able to complete the task. Start to finish the front windshield took us about 3 hours. Now the clean up. My fingers were a mess with black goop all over me; and my sweatshirt was trash. Paul had a little on his hands and a couple racing stripes on his sweatshirt. Dennis remained Mr. Clean.

We turned our attention to the rear glass and spent several hours pushing and tugging and squeezing and scratching our heads, but we just couldn't get the back window into the new rubber gasket. We tried the old gasket and had it partially installed but it was so tired and torn that it just looked terrible so we stopped to think some more. We placed a call to Mr. Congeniality who went crawling up into his garage attic for us. Aha! His windshield was only 1/8" thick whereas mine was ¼". Therefore we concluded we had the wrong gasket or the wrong window. Seeing as how this was the only gasket available for a Europa, I made the trip down to Lyons that night and traded Bill one thick rear window for a thin one. He's not going to use a rear window on his Europa Del Sol anyway. More of a flow through ventilation. Thanks Bill!

The next day I attacked the rear window again but couldn't quite get the stiff new gasket to accept the somewhat flimsy new/old glass. As I was pushing on the glass I was really afraid that the flimsy thing would just shatter and I would be spewing red blood on my red car. Not wishing to do this I cleaned up Bill's original gasket which was not bad and slipped that into place. After a lot of pushing and squeezing and contortions, I had the rear glass in the old gasket in about 2 hours. Success – or at least partial success! I then started working on the locking bead that gets inserted into the middle of the rubber all the way around the glass. That I could do up to a point. I got the bottom part fished through but could not make the turn. It was just too tight of a turn. I tried the top and found that I could get the straight part in but again could not make the turn. So if you look at the installed window now real close you may notice that the locking strip is installed all the way around except the right side which has a little bead of black silicone. Looks fine and it will never fall out. I remember now that when I got the car originally from Rich it did not have any locking strip at all so things should be OK. After 8 hours in the garage working on that stupid rear glass my fingers were so sore I could barely pop the top on a cold one – but I did!

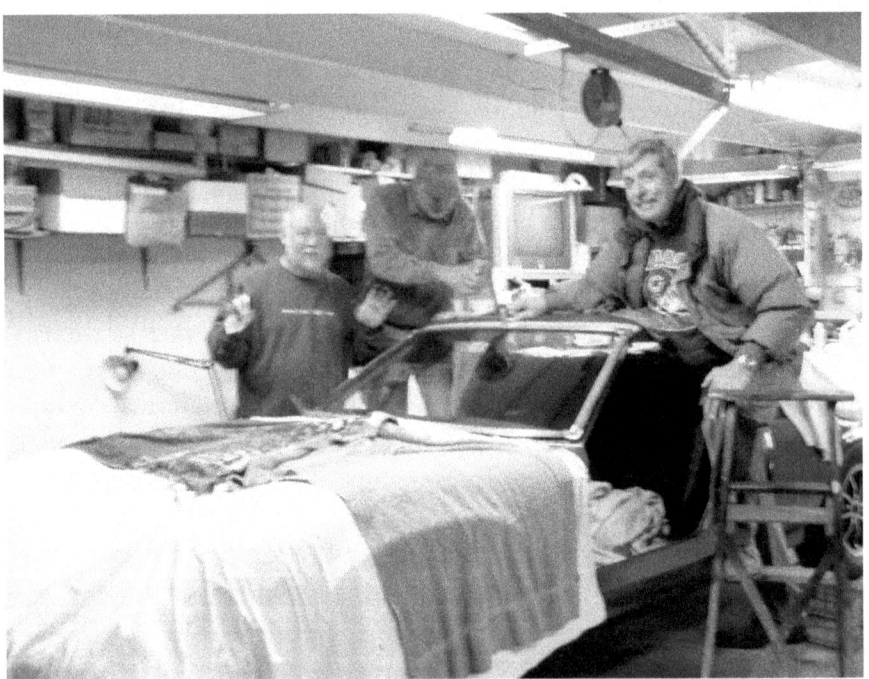

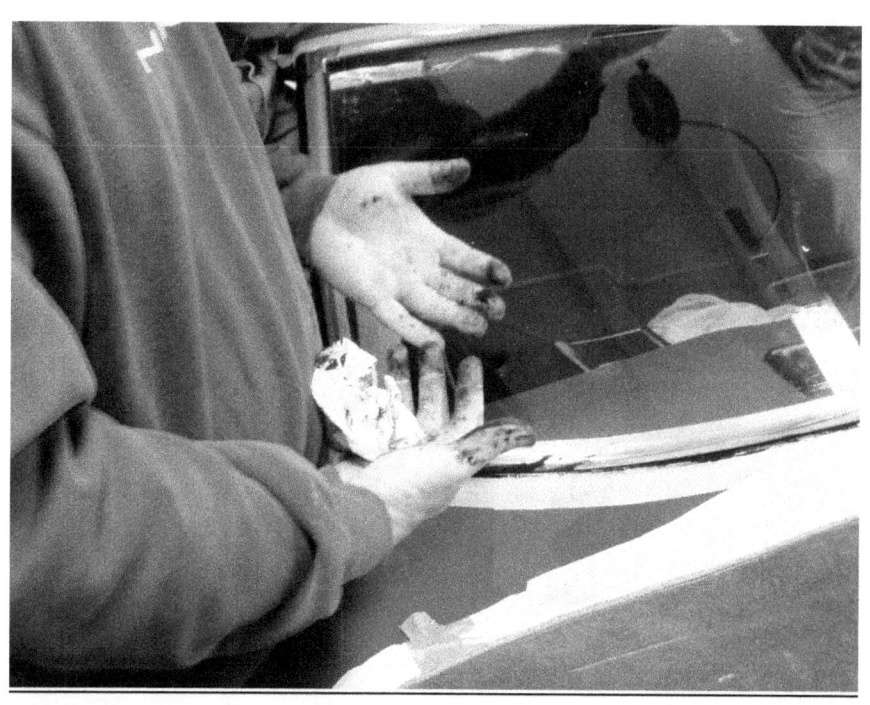
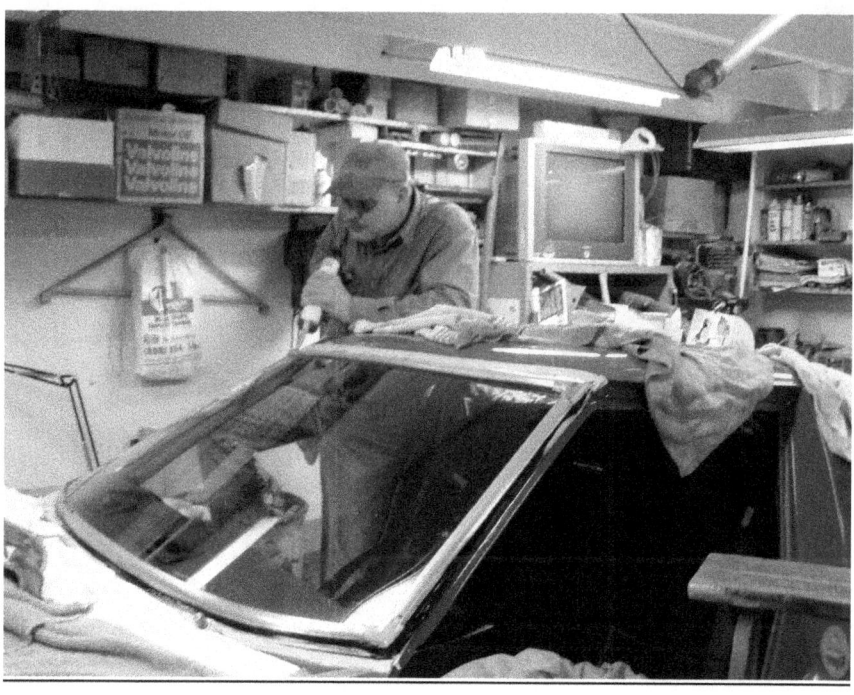

Europa Euphoria by Bob Herzog Part 30 of?

The hood and the trunk lid (or boot and bonnet) posed no real interesting challenge. The steel engine venting grates took a lot of scrubbing with a wire brush to clean up. A rattle can spritz of chrome paint made them look like new! Next up was the removable rear trunk which was pretty beat up with several splits and tears here and there. I spent a Saturday with some fiberglass followed by a little Bondo repairing all the cracks and making it look good. I finished up by giving it a spritz of truck bed liner paint. Nice! I mounted the stock air cleaner to the back of the removable trunk (yes, that's where it goes) and mounted a small new fire extinguisher in the trunk as well.

On to the doors! A little sanding and rubbing was in order to get rid of the orange peel. I then had to figure out how all the rods and gizzies fit inside the door to make the door open, close and lock as well as how to mount the power window motor. The motors were a bit grungy and took a bit of cleaning over the garbage can with brake clean, followed by a liberal application of white grease out of the spray can. By the way, don't get your face too close to a part you are spraying with white grease – it doesn't sting your eyes but it also does not clean up real easy with soap and water. Somehow I found that out – the hard way.

I assembled door number one and then taped off its edges along with the edges of the door opening. I summoned the spousal unit and she assisted me with the installation. I held the door in place and she hammered the hinge shaft up from the hole in the bottom of the car up through the two stainless steel hinges and up into it's home pocket in the top of the door opening. These are nice new stainless steel parts covered with a nice coating of white grease so they should not rust out for ever, or at least not for a few months until I sell the car which is good enough for me. Anyway, we had success on the first try and the door actually lined up and opens and closes and everything – terrifical!

The Lotus Corps tune up clinic was coming up and I had set a goal to actually drive the Europa there. It didn't really have to be 100% done but I did want a nice presentation. So I had been working on a number of things to get it ready. I glued the rear view mirror back on as it might be nice to see out the back. On a similar note I mounted the side view mirrors which had somehow been painted red to match the car somewhere along the way. Looked pretty good. I finally decided it was time to see if we had all the pieces together for some forward zoom so one evening after work I dropped the car off the milk crates she had been sitting on for about 6 months. I cranked down on the battery cutoff switch bringing full voltages to bear. I squeezed myself into the cockpit - that's about the size of it too, a pit just big enough for a good sized….. Rooster – what did you think I was going to say? Well Cock a doodle doo! I had forgotten how much fun it was to get into a Europa. It used to be a lot easier 20 years ago before I grew a bowling ball in my stomach. You put your right leg in, kind of drop yourself down, plopping your buttocks into the seat. You then arch your back and scrunch your head down to clear the door opening. All's well until you realize that your left leg is still dangling outside the car and it don't bend back on a 45 degree angle to the left which is what's required to enter. That requires some manual pulling and grunting but finally – I'm in. Even remembered to bring the key! Cranked her over and she fired up easily enough and with a little coaxing of the choke got her to idle OK. A bit high but we'll deal with that later. I pushed in the clutch however and could not find any gear – hmmmmm. It was like the gates were blocked or like the clutch was not disengaging – hmmmmm. I shut her down and engaged the spousal unit to ensure that the clutch cable was connected to the clutch lever. How come she has no problem getting in and out of the Europa? (I'm glad that she has taken good care of herself over the years and does not have a bowling ball growth like I do.) Upon depression of the pedal it was confirmed that I was indeed getting sufficient clutch arm throw – hmmmm. I dismissed the spousal unit to go about the rest of her mundane evening and got out the wrenches and adjusted the clutch from all the way loose (which was where I figured a new clutch should be adjusted) to all the way tight. Once back inside the pit I could feel that I was absolutely bottoming out the pressure plate when I depressed the pedal but yet I could still not find a gear when the car was running – hmmmm. I shut her off and put her in gear and started it up again. She started creeping forward and was difficult to pull out of gear. At least the brakes seemed to work OK. I shut it down again and did a rewind of the trans/clutch/pressure plate assembly process in my mind. Didn't even need a 12 oz. can of rewind fluid as I was still quite determined to drive around the block one way or another. Something was still hanging up in the clutch department but I wanted to go – so I just did. Started her up in first gear and out of the garage we crept. I let out the clutch and it engaged the rest of the way just fine. I cruised down the ally and cautiously turned the corner right into a gaggle of soccer moms in their mini vans going to some school function at the corner grade school. Lots of funny looks as I gently negotiated the traffic and made a turn down my street. Once clear of traffic I attempted a shift but only got it to come out of gear, but it did not want to go into 2nd. I pulled over, shut her off, put her in gear, restarted and finished my one block lap waving at Paul's neighbor lady Hazel at the corner. Over the 25 years I've been testing cars out around the block I always seem to catch Hazel sitting outside or walking about. She always gives me a funny look like what the heck is he driving now? Nice lady!

So I made it around the block and pushed the Europa back into the garage, but after conferring with my SME (Paul) we decided that the new pilot bearing I had installed was probably a bit undersized due to me pressing it into place. We decided that if I tried to let it "wear in" I would run the risk of it overheating, gnarling up and locking up the bearing. So it was time to pull the trans back out – what fun!

4 hours out and 4 hours in is about what it took. That's skipping all the details which included a few cuts, split nails and some cursing. Bottom line, the problem was that the input shaft bearing that mounts in the flywheel was sticking out maybe 1/16 of an inch instead of being flush. Why? Have no clue. I'll have to fire the mechanic again. While the trans was out I spent a little time with some sandpaper to make sure both the input bearing and the input shaft were free of boogars and that the bearing indeed spun freely on the shaft even after it was mounted on the flywheel. All is well now!

I finished up buttoning up everything and fired her up. This time I was able to find a gear, but only 1st, second and reverse – hmmmmmm? But I took a couple laps around the block anyway – more progress. Now upon further investigation I found a worn pivot bushing for the shift shaft.. Seemed OK when apart but with all the leverage of the long shift arm that goes from the shifter in the middle of the car, all the way back to the back of the trans at the very back of the car, that bushing needed to be a whole lot tighter. So I spent an hour down by Paul's while he used his 1940's lathe to hog out the bushings to the next larger size so I could use a 5/16 inch bolt instead of a ¼ inch. Let's try this again

I put everything back together but got the same results. Reverse is too easy, 1st and second is where 3 & 4 should be and no 3 or 4 or 5. Time to bring in the insulting consultants. Luckily there was a Lotus Corps Bored meeting scheduled for my house the following evening. Plied with some cold beverages I should be able to extract some knowledge to attain un-stuckness once more!

Carl Sarro, Rich Cwik and Paul Quiniff all converged on the Europa. They inspected, poked around, discussed theories and generally agreed that something was out of adjustment. Rich quickly found the section in the manual where the adjustment procedures were documented. We had to break up the frivolity to attend the meeting but at least I had a clue where to start the following day.

I started reading the manual (it happens) and found a pretty good description of what to do when you replace a bunch of parts in the trans which I had not done. After all the adjustments are made however you are supposed to drill and pin the little reverse detent cam so that the linkage only goes into 1/2/3/4 unless you push it past the detent into either reverse in one direction of the detent, or 5th gear in the other direction of the detent. After further reflection it became apparent that I had the little cam in upside down. I had a 50/50 chance of getting it right the first time as it looks the same either way. I must had flipped the cam upon reassembly. I dropped the trans. a bit to get at the pin, pulled it out with vice grips and reinstalled the cam the opposite way. I put everything back together, dropped her down and squeezed back into the cockpit. AHA – there's those missing gears! Fired it up and took her around the block a few times using 1st through 4th. Couldn't find 5th yet but this is progress. Time to celebrate with some fluids – but not beer! I drove her to the corner gas station and filled the dual aluminum tanks with $25 of premium fuel. Nothing but the best for this beast who is finally starting to be tamed!

Europa Euphoria by Bob Herzog Part 31 of?

On the lower part of the sills on each side of the Europa Twin cam there is a metal strip and a fiberglass valence. The stock color of the valence is a very bright metal flake silver. Kind of a 70's Disco ball silver. The panels that came with this car were a bit beat up so I spent some time grinding down the cracks, tears and chips and repairing them properly with fiberglass. I followed this up with a little Bondo and some sanding to get everything smooth and looking good. A nice coat of primer followed by some spot putty and some more primer and they were ready for color. I didn't have any silver paint in stock so I tried a rattle can from Auto Zone and it turned out horrible. Sanded that off and stopped by Advance auto parts one day to find a quart can of Duplicolor pre-mixed silver metal flake ON SALE at half off. If it was regular price I would have just bought it. But because it was a close out sale I had to read it and inspect it and finally decided all was well so I bought it. Turned out fine, just really settled so it took a lot of shaking and stirring to get those flakes all evenly mixed up. I set up the panels on a table outside as it was a nice dry sun shiny day and I didn't feel like taking out the cars and covering things up in the garage. The silver shot real nice and glistened in the sun. I followed up with some clear coat and crossed my fingers that no bugs would decide to do the back stroke in the clear pool of clear coat. About an hour later I was talking with my son John as I exited the garage and I saw a Dove hovering about 5 feet off the table. It was almost in slow motion that I yelled NO!!!! and the Dove quickly turned in mid air and flew away. I don't know if he would have landed in the clear or on the clear coat but I was glad he missed and I brought the still tacky panels into the garage to dry overnight.

The next day they went on easily enough. A self tapping screw or two at each end holding the ends onto the fiberglass fender lips. Now there is a visual image – a fender with lips…Anyway, the top of these panels is simply held on with one long strip of double stick tape. The stainless steel strip that runs across the top of them is held on with little metal clips which are riveted to the body. It works and looks pretty good when I finished it all up.

Back to my missing 5th gear. I knew where it was – in the transmission. It's just that the shift linkage didn't want to go there. I set up shop at the back of the trans with my Polish creeper (an old carpet) and a drop light. I laid on my side and inspected and poked around and twisted the linkage back and forth trying to figure out what was not quite right. After a while the G-forces of laying on my side without support for my fat head put a strain on neck so I got up and found a suitable head support device. An old but clean oil drain pan flipped upside down did the trick. Now I was able to investigate and contemplate without having to hold up my head. Of course, in walks the spousal unit. She stops at my feet, surveys my situation and says something like what the H E Double Hockey sticks are you doing? Are you crazy? Using a dirty oil drain pan for a pillow? Hey, it's clean I told her. Well, pretty clean.

After poking around a bit, I surmised that I had two minor adjustment problems. The first one was that the detent that pushes against the ball was a bit worn so the detent would not push the ball into the hole. It was just trying to push against the ball sideways. I took out the detent cam and fabricated a little metal strip covering out of 10 thou steel and epoxied it in place. The other piece to this puzzle was that even though the cam was pinned in place, the hole where the pin went was a bit sloppy so the cam could actually pivot a bit until you clamped down the locking nut. Thus as I tightened the lock nut, the cam moved out of adjustment. What was required was a big channel lock pliers to hold the cam in place as I locked down the lock nut. Now I could feel an even side to side movement and when I moved the shift arm one way, the detent moved enough to get into reverse, and when I moved it the other way, it felt like that should be the missing 5th gear! I dropped her down and got everything ready for a trip to my interior guy the next morning.

Kn'S's in Des Plaines does nice interior work and I had scheduled to drop the car off Tuesday morning after the Memorial day weekend. Since his shop is right by the train station in downtown Des Plaines I just took my laptop case with me in the Europa so I could catch the train to work in downtown Chicago. A real commuter car. I wonder when was the last time this car was driven to work?

So anyways I pulled the Europa out of the garage and off I went. Morning rush hour traffic was a mess (yes, even in beautiful downtown Des Plaines) but I did manage to find all the gears including 5th on my short drive to Ken's. Ah, success! One bug down.

I dropped the car off with Ken. He had previously done the new seats and modified the Banks Europa crash pad for me. Both (all three?) of which were already in the car. Now he was going to do some finishing details like the headliner, vinyl coverings for the a-pillars and more vinyl around the rear window. He was also going to make me a new center arm rest pad and door insert along with new sun visors as the old ones were very petrified and he refused to let me put something old and crappy in a nicely done new interior. The cruddy old sun visors might have Cooties!

Europa Euphoria by Bob Herzog Part 32 of?

I picked up the car from Ken the interior guy (great work as usual) and began working away at the couple small but pesky bugs still left in the car. I had sent out the Tach and Speedo to MoMa in Albuquerque for a rebuild. The tach had worked somewhat before but it hung up after 3K. The Speedo worked but the tripometer did not. MoMa did a perfect rebuild job. Every thing looked great and worked great. In fact they changed the guts on the tach to a modern set up so it will work if the next owner changes from points to an electronic ignition. The tach and speedo went back in with some effort as there is absolutely no room to work under the dash. I had to run a new wire back to the coil as the new tach set up called for a straight wire instead of one in a series loop.

Since I had gotten this project Europa three years ago I had been looking and looking on ebay for a couple missing items. I got them all except one side badge and bezel that goes in the back along the side of the car. For our 25th wedding anniversary, my Son Mike and his wife got me a $100 gift certificate to Dave Bean. They also got a gift certificate for Sue to some type of Bed, Bath and Beyond a man's comprehension store. It will take Sue six months to get around spending that certificate. I was on the phone the next day spending all $100 of mine. They even gave me a little discount so that the badge, bezel, tax and delivery were exactly $100. Nice! I glued it on with clear silicone; hope it doesn't fall off!

On to the remaining bugs. One of the electrical glitches really had me going. Both the fuel gauge and the water temp gauge did not work. In reading up on things in the Europa Knowledgebase on the web I found that the usual suspect was the voltage stabilizer. It was actually not too bad to get at under the dash on the passenger side so I pulled it out for access. This issue had me scratching my head as it was supposed to read 12 volts in and 10 volts out (the regulator, not my head). What I got was 12 volts in and a pulsing voltage out? What the heck? Am I hooked up to the turn signals? Upon further review in all the comments regarding voltage stabilizers on the web I found that this was Lucas normal. There is normal and then there is Lucas normal. The Lucas voltage stabilizer is actually more of a voltage averager. It pulses between 12 and 6 volts with the gauges responding slow enough that it averaged at 10 volts. Whatever – it's Lucas technology. So mine was OK. So I had to find out what else the problem could be. I took off the water temp lead and grounded it. I stuck my head in the cockpit to have a look as this should have made the water gauge peg but it didn't move. I scratched my head, mumbled a few things and as I was exiting the cockpit I noticed that the fuel gauge was pegged – Hmmmmmmmm! Seems that there was a wire reversed somewhere in the harness under the dash. Right where it was impossible to get at. So I reversed the wires back in the engine bay. That made it so the temp gauge now worked. After much more diagnosis and running of extra ground leads, I determined that alas, the gas sending unit was kaput. And since the gauge was basically swinging inside the tank I decided that the next owner could just fill up every 250 miles and reset the tripometer instead of me jacking up the car 4 feet, draining the tank and dropping the left tank for easy access.

   A couple more short trips to see what else is not quite right and I think I'm done!

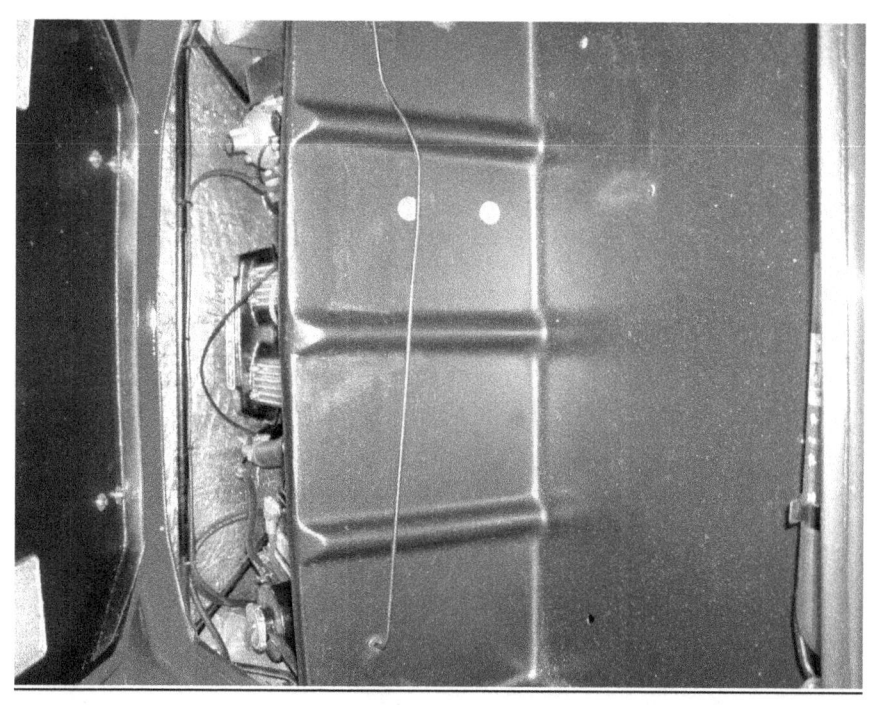

Europa Euphoria by Bob Herzog Part 33 of?

Now comes the next challenge, selling the car. What price for all this work? No Europa is worth Ferrari bucks. But then again, this is a very nice Europa. Not many Europas have had a body off restoration. If you price it too high, you get a lot of laughs and crazy comments. If you price it too low, you lose out on some money. So I started high, placing an ad in the Lotus ReMarque for $29K and an ad in the Lotus Notus for $27K. There was an absolutely perfect Europa that sold on ebay a couple months ago for $32k. Then again, there are lots of them going for less than $10k.

No bites on the new Lotus newsletters so after a couple weeks there so I put an ad in the Sunday Chicago Tribune next. Got one call the first week and another the second. They both seemed interested but no bucks in my hand yet so to ebay I went. The first day I got 1,000 hits and 100 people watching along with 6 inquiries. One of them was interesting because the ebayer is French and you lose something with those translation web sites. Several emails back and forth on that one. I also spent about 45 minutes on the phone with a collector in Atlanta, answering all his questions. I had a starting price of $9,000 and a reserve of $21,000. You have a reasonable starting price so people will at least think about it. You set the reserve at what you really want for it. I rarely use a "buy it now" price, just in case I get something that several people with sufficient funds really want. Of course nobody bidding knows what the reserve is until a bidder hits it. Let the bidding begin!

All sorts of questions and comments ensued. I was really optimistic as at the end of the auction I had over 4500 hits and 185 watchers. But alas, they were watchers and not players as the bidding fizzled out at $15,000. I think all the other Europa owners in the world were trying to justify their own car's worth by sending me emails of how much they liked my car and how much they thought it would sell for. I re-listed it in ebay a couple weeks later with a $17,000 reserve.

Not as many watchers this time but there were some new bidders. In the end however the high bid again fell short of my reserve. Now it's time to wait and see who was thinking about it but did not have the spare cash to quite pull the trigger on ebay. 3 days after the auction I got the email I was looking for. The high bidder from the auction was a savvy collector in Canada. Through emails he asked what I really wanted for the car and we struck a deal at $16,000. Not as much as I had hoped for but I really only have at most about $10,000 in the car including the $4,000 purchase price. I kept track of the hours and it all totaled up to about 1100 hours start to finish over a 3 year, 5 month period. So doing the math that works out to 26.82 hours a month of work. But if you subtract the 6 months I took off to work on Paul's Elan that works out to be 35 months or 31.42 hours per month of fun. As to how much I made on the project, $6k goes into 1100 hours and comes out $5.45 per hour. Not bad for a hobby. How many people go golfing week after week after week and shell out $20-80 a day for greens fees? Wouldn't they like to get all that money back and make $5 an hour on top of it? I like what I do.

   I had a real nice conversation with the new owner when he called one evening to firm up the plans of transferring the money and shipping the car. He is a Canadian car collector who owns among other cars an Esprit (nice), and a Viper (I won't hold that against him). He had just sold his S2 Europa because it was in need to a major $$ injection for an engine rebuild and a paint job when mine came on the market. Good timing for both of us.

   The money appeared in my bank account the next day and I awaited a call from his shipper to tell me when to expect a truck. A couple days later I got a call at work from the trucker. He was on the road coming up through Indiana, had to make a couple of stops and wanted to pick up the Europa that night. We had just gone through the aftermath of hurricane Ike and my town of Des Plaines and the surrounding area had many closed roads due to flooding. It was going to be a challenge to get the big rig to where I was at. We talked for a bit and I told him to call me at home when he was leaving his last stop in Northfield, about 15 miles away.

   The trucker called and I gave him directions to get through on one of the few open roads crossing the overflowing Des Plaines river. I agreed to meet him in the K-mart parking lot a few blocks away. A lot easier for loading. About 8:30 pm, I started up the Europa and headed on over. The rig was there already with the big ramps already down awaiting the tiny little Europa. This was a big open trailer truck towing another trailer. Looked to be 55' long? I don't know. It was as big as I've ever seen. The trucker was friendly and really liked to talk. After a bit I drove the Europa up the ramps. It barely cleared but barely is enough. He chained her down in the front and rear and then used the hydraulics to move the whole thing up and into the rig. He had a huge Ford truck precariously perched above the tiny little Europa and as he fiddled with his levers he brought down the Ford to within a few inches of the Europa nose. I guess it's his baby now. I signed the release, gave him the title and away he went. Off to Canada after one more stop on the South side of Chicago.

Europa Euphoria – by Bob Herzog Part 34 of 34

I got an email from the new owner who was happy with the car – which made we feel good. He cleaned the car up from the transport to Canada and took it to the Toronto British car festival. There were over 1,000 cars there including a lot of Lotus cars. In the Elan, Esprit, Europa and other category there were 40 cars and the Europa took first place!

Well, it's gone now, another project out the door. About 3 ½ years from the day Rich and I picked up the glow in the dark green Europa at Jack Buchinger's out in Princeton to the night that I drove the bright shiny red Europa up the big trailer ramps at the K-mart parking lot. The Europa was fun in some ways, challenging in others. There were times I would really be looking forward to getting out to the garage to work on her, other times I was considering getting a giant sledge hammer out and beating the car to death. Overall it turned out pretty good. Overall however Europas in general are not for me. They have too claustrophobic of an interior and the close windshield can make it too hot inside. This Europa did look very nice and ran very nice and it was something to be very proud of. I had brought another Lotus back from the dead but this will be my last Europa project.

This makes about the 7th total restoration I've done and about the 15th Lotus I've owned. I have an early Elan coupe project in bits and pieces all over the place and a 1965 Cortina Estate Wagon (The Lotus Cortina Shooting Brake) sitting under my porch in Des Plaines waiting for me. Here I go again!

About the cover……

When I was restoring the Europa I took some pictures with a digital camera that was only a couple years old. At the time, If you took high resolution pictures with a digital camera, you would have no place to put them as your computer would not hold that much. Fast forward 5 years and now almost all the pictures I took of the Europa were not of a high enough resolution for the front cover of this book. Therefore the picture on the cover of this book was not my first choice. The picture on the cover is that of a Europa model in my back yard. Here was my first choice:

To see all the restoration pictures and more, visit LotusCorps.org.

This page intentionally left blank.

This page left blank by mistake.

www.ingramcontent.com/pod-product-compliance
Lightning Source LLC
Chambersburg PA
CBHW061447040426
42450CB00007B/1260